THE GREAT COOKIE JAR

TAKING THE MYSTERIES OUT OF THE MONEY SYSTEM

THE GREAT COOKIE JAR

TAKING THE MYSTERIES OUT OF THE MONEY SYSTEM

by

Edward E. Popp

WISCONSIN EDUCATION FUND
P. O. Box 321
Port Washington, Wisconsin 53074

This book is dedicated
to all persons who produce and distribute
useful goods
and to all who render
useful services.
They are the producers of
the wealth of the nation.
May they learn how to issue and use
bona fide credit certificates as currency
so that inflation, deflation, balance of
payments deficits, and government debts
will have no good reason to exist!

Library of Congress Catalog Card Number: 78-62961
International Standard Book Number (ISBN)
0-960-0358-2-6

WISCONSIN EDUCATION FUND
P.O. Box 321 Port Washington
Wisconsin 53074

Manufactured in the United States of America

CONTENTS

INTRODUCTION

Movies and novels have made neural surgeons and nuclear physicists today's stereotype of the super-brain. Yet recently, when an informed high-school student sought to explain to a neural surgeon how money is brought into existence in the United States, his listener exclaimed. "Stop! That stuff is just too deep for me!"

Now, if an individual of that caliber thinks the subject of money is too deep, we might well ask how anyone could write a whole book about it and expect it to become a best-seller. Money, of course, is just about everyone's favorite subject; but that fact derives from all those wonderful things that money *buys*, not from the delights of contemplating such mechanisms as devaluation, inflation, balance of payments, and exchange ratios.

Incredibly, Dr. Edward Popp appears to have done the impossible. He has produced a scholarly study of money that should and *could* become a best-seller. His highly original work, *The Great Cookie Jar*, with its well-marshalled facts and irrefutable conclusions, is both a classic and a bombshell! It is a classic because no one else has told us in such simple, step-by-step fashion, just what money is, how it is brought into existence, and what the results of this method of money-creation are. It is a bombshell because Dr. Popp goes further. He shows us that our money is essentially the equivalent of *counterfeit!* He explains how it happened and who it is that has a monopolistic right to create our money out of nothing—and then collect interest on it. When the cookie jar is the whole money system, we have a right to know who has his hand in it; and if you think it is the government, then you had better think again!

For decades the reasons behind the cyclical spectacle of monetary depressions have been couched under such familiar headings as "economic uncertainty," "trade imbalances," "excessive public debt," "deflationary pressures," "overheating of the economy," "expansion of the money supply," and "runaway inflation." These phrases tend to obscure rather than clarify just what is going on. Few of us have understood, *really understood,* just what they mean; nor have we been highly motivated to learn. Just like our friend the surgeon, we have harbored the suspicion that "that stuff's just too deep for me."

Well, enter sunshine, enter illumination, enter easy, delightful and exciting understanding! In a word, enter Dr. Popp! His incredibly informative, totally absorbing, and topically complete treatment of the subject of money simply has no equal. This is one of those *once in a century* books that delivers a fresh, revealing, accurate, and co-ordinated picture of an entire subject-matter, and does so at the level of common understanding.

Above all, Dr. Popp doesn't leave us stranded. While not one person in ten thousand understands our present money system and not one in a million understands what a proper money system *should* be, only the most rare theoretician understands how to get from where we *are* to where we *ought to be* without producing global disaster in the process. Dr. Popp is the articulate spokesman of that elitist circle.

I predict that the simple substance of *The Great Cookie Jar* will emerge as the primary position in the political platform of every party in America that is seriously concerned with the re-establishment of Constitutional principles and an economy of material abundance. I predict that responsible patriots in every nation on earth will then echo that American example. And I hold—I don't know if we yet dare predict—that the clear concepts presented in *The Great Cookie Jar* eventually will become embodied in a fundamental educational course, not in the graduate schools, not in the colleges, nor even in the high-schools of America, but in the grammar-schools all across this great land.

What a fantastic vision of hope and creativity this unique book reveals! It opens vistas largely undreamed of and truly unknown. I recommend it wholeheartedly.

G. Edward Griffin
President, American Media

June, 1978

PREFACE

This book was written to give students and others a more detailed explanation of some of the items discussed in textbooks on money and banking. An introduction to the subject is given in my first book, *Money—Bona Fide or Non-Bona Fide*. In addition to a general expansion on the topics discussed in the previous text, the present work includes a study of effects on the economy of the fractional reserve banking system and the operations of the Federal Open Market Committee.

The word "dollar" is frequently used, and yet, few know its origin and the different meanings people apply to it. Debts are accepted as if it is normal for people and governmental bodies to be perpetually in debt. Few writers warn us of the evils of debts and almost no one tells us how to avoid incurring them.

Today we find ourselves overwhelmed with money problems such as inflation, deflation, government debts and balance of payments deficits. These problems are not caused by ineptitude or wrongdoing on the part of the producers and the distributors of goods and services, nor are they caused by the private enterprise system. Neither are they accidental.

These problems are created principally by the widespread use of what is called bank credit. Textbooks call it credit, credit money, money, or money supply. It is a substitute for bona fide coins, bona fide credit certificates, or bona fide warehouse receipts which could be used as media of exchange.

We have been led to believe that the items that serve as media of exchange are scarce and can be obtained only by borrowing them and paying interest for their use. I have tried to disprove that assumption and to propose a better system. To improve our money system it is neither necessary nor wise to destroy our present system. It is only necessary to produce a better product and to introduce it gradually. For nearly six hundred years the government of England issued and used a bona fide currency without the use of gold or silver and without borrowing it. We can do the same.

We can issue enough interest-free bona fide currency so that the commercial banks can operate on a 100% reserve banking system for demand deposits, thus preventing the banking system from legally inflating or deflating the money supply.

It is easy to see that there is something wrong when we have to incur such enormous interest-bearing debts just to have sufficient media of exchange for the normal exchanging of our goods and services. These burdensome debts, especially the debts incurred by governmental bodies, are the result of the use of bank credit as our principal medium of exchange.

This is an interesting and timely subject. I hope the viewpoints I present will stimulate greater interest in a field that demands more broadly based knowledge.

Edward E. Popp

Port Washington
Wisconsin 53074

CHAPTER I

WORDS MUST HAVE DEFINITE MEANINGS

Ideas can be conveyed correctly only when the words used to express ideas have definite meanings. When a teacher wishes to teach a subject he must use words that have a precise meaning and he must do everything he can to make sure that his students understand that meaning.

In textbooks and other reading matter on money and banking we find many words with vague meanings. This is why the subject of money and banking is spoken of as being complicated or difficult to understand. If people call something by a name other than what it is, that does not make it the thing it is called. Let us explain by telling a story. A farmer asked his son,

"Son, how many legs has a horse?"

The son replied, "Four."

"Correct," said the father. "Now if we call the horse's tail a leg, then how many legs will the horse have?"

"Five," said the boy.

"You're wrong," said the father. "The horse still has only four legs. Just because we call the tail a leg does not make the tail a leg."

The student may wish to keep that story in mind when he is reading his textbooks on money and banking. He will probably find that many words, especially the word "money," are used ambiguously. So I shall start out by giving my definition of the word "money."

The word "money" has its origin from the word "mint." The Latin word for mint is *moneta*. The same word, "moneta," in Latin means a coin. Words such as "monetary," and "monetize" are derived from the Latin word "moneta."

Similarly, in Old English the word for mint was "mynet," which in addition to signifying the place where coins were produced, meant the coins themselves. As the English language changed, mynet became mynit, then mynyt, and finally mint. In Middle English the word was changed to moneye, and later it became "money."

Article I, Section 8 of the United States Constitution states, "The Congress shall have Power . . . to coin money . . ." The verb "to coin" means to make coins. So, when the writers of the Constitution used the word "money," the word "money" meant coins.

The phrase "to coin money" did not and does not mean to print or to issue United States notes. If the writers of the Constitution wanted Congress to have the power to issue United States notes in addition to the power to make coins, they would have stated that fact in the following words: The Congress shall have the power to coin money and to emit Bills (as it was written in the Articles of Confederation) or Bills of Credit (as they wrote it in Article I, Section 10, of the United States Constitution). Those were the terms the people used at that time to mean government-issued unredeemable notes which were intended to be used as currency.

Thus, we conclude that the word "money" originally meant coins, especially the coins made by a government-owned mint. The word "money" included gold, silver, and base metal coins.

As time passed, gold and silver certificates and bank notes were issued and were redeemed with gold or silver coins. Because the paper certificates and notes were interchangeable with coins and served the same purpose as coins (money), people began to call them paper money, and in recent years, just money. But calling notes and certificates money did not make them money (coins).

If we would use the word "money" to mean coins, and only coins, no ambiguity would exist.

Just because items other than coins are used as media of exchange does not mean that we have to call those items money. If we were to pay for something with postage stamps we would not call the postage stamps money. Likewise, if other documents such as notes, checks or certificates are used as media of exchange we should not call them money. Each item should be called what it is. Collectively they may be called items that serve as media of exchange.

BILLS OF EXCHANGE

The following documents are bills of exchange: checks, drafts, warrants, money orders, and perhaps other items. Bills of exchange are written orders from one party to another to pay a certain sum to a third party. They are issued by the owner of the sum to be paid. Therefore they are self limiting and their issuance places no one in debt. The issuer can never honestly issue more than the amount of funds he owns. Because they are self limiting their issuance will never cause an inflation of the media of exchange. The amount that may be issued never needs to be controlled by the government or by the Federal Reserve System. Note that Article I, Section 10 of the Constitution which says, "No State shall . . . emit Bills of Credit," does not say, No State shall emit Bills of Exchange.

BILLS OF CREDIT

A law dictionary defines a bill of credit as follows: "Paper issued by the authority of the state on the faith of the state, and designed to circulate as money." I would say that the meanings of the word "paper" and the phrase "on the faith of the state," and even the word "money" are ambiguous and therefore inappropriate in a definition.

That definition would be more meaningful if it read as follows: A bill of credit is a document, or a note, issued by government officials, such as the former United

States notes, or by the authority of government officials, such as the former Federal Reserve notes, with a promise to pay coins or other currency which the issuer does not have, and designed to circulate as currency.

But in addition to written promises to pay currency that the issuer does not have, commercial banks extend bank credit (verbal promises to pay more cash than they have) that serves as written bills of credit.

When governmental bodies and banks issue promises to pay coins or other currency which they do not have, the amount of the promises (notes or bank credit) that they can issue is not self limiting. Perhaps that is why those who wish to control the money supply say that money will not manage itself. If we would use only honestly issued redeemable notes or certificates as media of exchange the money supply would manage itself because every item issued would be self limiting.

The use of bills of credit and their equivalent, bank credit, as media of exchange since 1694 has taught us that both are very unsatisfactory media of exchange. At times their use has given us prosperity but it has also brought money panics, bank failures, inflation, deflation, booms and busts. The important thing that we should have learned from the use of unredeemable notes and unredeemable bank credit, however, is that it is necessary to increase continually the total debts of the country in order to have sufficient media of exchange. Without debts the notes and/or bank credit would not exist and without the notes and/or bank credit enough media of exchange would not exist.

The individual states have not issued any notes (bills of credit) since the Constitution was ratified in 1791. The United States government issued notes (bills of credit) only in 1862 and 1863. Various banks, however, have issued and loaned out notes which served as media of exchange from colonial times until about 1936. Since 1936 only the Federal Reserve banks have issued notes which serve as media of exchange. Between 1936 and 1965 the Federal Reserve notes were supposed to be redeemable in lawful money, but in practice they were only exchangeable for other currency. Since 1965 the Federal Reserve notes no longer contain the written promise "Redeemable in Lawful Money." In practice, they still are exchangeable for coins.

Because the commercial banks operate their demand deposit accounts on a fractional reserve basis, bank credit is loaned out to serve as media of exchange just as if it were bills of credit or bank notes. The effects are the same with one important exception. When the government issued bills of credit, no interest was charged. When banks issue bills of credit (notes) or its equivalent, bank credit, interest is always charged. (The fractional reserve system is explained in chapter XI.)

GOLD AND SILVER CERTIFICATES

Gold and silver certificates were documents giving evidence that gold or silver was on deposit in the treasury of the United States and that it was payable to the bearer on demand. They were self limiting and no interest-bearing debt resulted from their issuance. They were a combination of a warehouse receipt and a certificate of legal tender.

CERTIFICATES OF CREDIT

Certificates of credit (gift certificates) are documents usually issued by merchants which give evidence that the bearer has a claim for a certain number of dollars' worth of goods owned by the issuer. Only a relatively small amount of them are being used as media of exchange. They are self limiting and no interest-bearing debt is created when they are issued. Bona fide certificates of credit, issued in convenient denominations, could serve as a very practical medium of exchange.

WAREHOUSE RECEIPTS

A warehouse receipt is similar to a certificate of credit

except that it gives evidence of a claim for a certain quantity of goods (pounds, tons, gallons, etc.) instead of dollars' worth of the items. They, too, are self limiting and no interest-bearing debt is incurred when they are issued. A warehouse receipt serves very well as a store of value and to some extent as a medium of exchange.

Let us keep in mind that in order to issue a bona fide warehouse receipt or a certificate of credit that is redeemable in gold, silver or other goods, somebody must be the keeper of the goods. Only the keeper of the goods can issue demand claims against the goods and he must be willing to give up the goods when the demand claims are presented to him. He cannot, therefore, issue demand claims for more goods than he possesses.

TAX CREDIT CERTIFICATES

Tax credit certificates are government-issued documents giving evidence that they will be received as payment for all fees, fines, dues and other charges due the government, and that they will be redeemed when they are presented as payment for the taxes levied at the time they were issued. They could be issued and used as payment for the needed government expenses. If they are issued in convenient denominations they would serve very well as media of exchange. They are self limiting and no interest-bearing debts are incurred when they are issued.

PAPER MONEY

When a writer uses the term "paper money," the reader has no way of knowing what the writer means by the term. He may mean any of the many documents which might serve as media of exchange. He may mean gold or silver certificates, Federal Reserve notes, United States notes or other bank notes. All of these notes and certificates are paper documents. But there is a great difference between these documents, even though they may all serve as media of exchange. I suggest, to avoid confusion, that we call each document what it is and not use the term "paper money."

LAWFUL MONEY

Once we accept the definition of the word "money" as coins, it is obvious that the term "lawful money" means lawfully made coins. It does not mean notes or certificates.

Formerly, when Federal Reserve notes were redeemable in lawful money, it meant that the notes were supposed to be redeemable in lawfully made coins. From 1914 to 1933 it meant lawfully made United States gold coins. Since 1934 Federal Reserve notes may be exchanged, but not redeemed, for lawfully made circulating United States coins. To redeem a note means to destroy the note. On page 50 in *The Constitution of the United States: Its Sources and Its Application*[1] by Thomas J. Norton, we read

> . . . the Act of Congress of February 25, 1862, as revised down to March 3, 1863, is still effective, declaring that "United States notes shall be lawful money, and a legal tender in payment of all debts, public and private, within the United States, except for duties on imports and interest on the public debts."

When we read that quotation we should remember that just because the Congress declared United States notes to be lawful money, the notes did not become lawful money, i.e., they did not become lawfully made coins. We also should keep in mind that the Constitution did not give Congress the power to emit bills of credit or to declare anything to be a legal tender.

---

[1]The following quotations from Thomas James Norton's *The Constitution of the United States: Its Sources and Its Application*, are used by the permission and courtesy of The Committee for Constitutional Government, 71 West 23rd. Street, New York, New York 10010.

LEGAL TENDER

The term "legal tender" has a different meaning from the term "lawful money." Legal tender is a legal quality applied by a governmental body to any item of currency it so designates. Any item which the governmental body authorizes a debtor to tender (to offer) and requires a creditor to receive as payment for money obligations is *called* legal tender. But, in order for an item to really be legal tender, the governmental body must have the authority to make such a law.

For example, in 1933 Congress without the authority from the United States Constitution applied legal tender qualities to Federal Reserve notes, which formerly were not legal tender, and declared gold coins, which formerly were legal tender, to be illegal. Despite the fact that before 1933 Federal Reserve notes were not legal tender and not declared to be lawful money, they circulated as currency. However, they were receivable "for all taxes, customs and other public dues." That fact was written on each note.

EXPLANATION

When a governmental body declares an item of currency to be legal tender, people naturally regard that currency as the best that can be devised. History has taught us that many unjust settlements of debts have been made with legal tender. Legal tender laws serve to legitimize an inflation of the currency. While legal tender laws are not needed, however, no injustice would result if Article 1, Section 10 of the Constitution were followed. The states then could declare government-issued gold and silver coins to be legal tender at the market value of their metal content at the time the coins were used as a payment.

In Article 1, Section 10 of the United States Constitution we read the following: "No State shall make any Thing but gold and silver coin a tender in Payment of debts." That is the only provision in the Constitution wherein a governmental body is permitted to make anything a legal tender.

We know that if the states declared gold and silver coins issued either by the United States government or by a foreign government to be legal tender, they could with honesty declare the coins to be legal tender only for an exchange value equal to the market value of their metal content at the time the coins were used as a payment. They could not declare them legal tender at the time they were minted or after they were used as a payment. The states were declaring foreign gold and silver coins legal tender at the time the Constitution was being written and that is what they did until 1857. Many Mexican silver coins, for example, circulated in the United States until 1857.

The writers of the Constitution knew that inflations of the currency occurred because the Continental Congress and the states had declared the Continental currency and state-issued bills of credit to be legal tender.

In 1923 the people in Germany experienced many unjust settlements of debts because the Reichbank's notes were declared to be legal tender.

LEGAL TENDER LAWS IN THE UNITED STATES

Let us give some background information to show how changeable and unpredictable the legal tender laws have been in our own country because our government officials did not follow Article I, Section 10 of the Constitution. If the Constitution were followed, the legal tender laws would never change unless the Constitution itself were changed.

When our government officials do not follow Article I, Section 10 of the Constitution, the people who sign contracts for future payments to be made in legal tender cannot be sure of the exchange value of that future payment. It may or may not be a just payment. The members of Congress surely did not receive from the Constitution or from any other source the right to pass laws to legalize unjust settlement of debts.

The Coinage Act of 1792 made all United States gold and silver coins legal tender at their face value for payment in any amount. In 1857 all laws which made foreign coins legal tender in the United States were repealed.

From 1879 to 1933 silver coins in fifty-cent, twenty-five cent and ten-cent demoninations were legal tender in one payment only for amounts up to ten dollars and five-cent and one-cent coins were legal tender in one payment only for amounts up to twenty-five cents. Silver dollar coins remained legal tender for payments in any amount from 1792 to the present time. Gold coins were legal tender for payments in any amount from 1792 to 1933. Since 1933 gold coins have not been legal tender.

United States notes were first issued on February 25, 1862. They were declared by Congress to be legal tender for all debts, public and private, at the time they were issued. After March 3, 1863, they were declared to be legal tender for all debts, public and private, except for payment of customs duties or payment of interest on the national debt.

On May 12, 1933, United States notes were made full legal tender for all payments, including customs duties and interest on the national debt.

On June 5, 1933, all United States coins except gold coins, and all other United States currency including, for the first time, Federal Reserve notes were declared to be legal tender for debts, public and private, for payments in any amount.

In 1935, however, the Supreme Court declared the June 5, 1933 Joint Resolution of Congress to be unconstitutional as applied to the payment of government bonds because it attempted to override the obligations agreed to in the bonds.

Let us give a little historical background information by again quoting from Thomas James Norton's book, *The Constitution of the United States: Its Sources and Its Application*[2]

---

[2]Pages 48-49

The Articles of Confederation forbade Congress to borrow or "emit bills" unless "nine States assent to the same." It was too often impossible to secure the support of that many. Hence this National power in our Constitution, which is entirely independent of State will.

In the Constitutional Convention the words "or emit bills," following the word "money" in the foregoing clause, were stricken out. Bills of credit or paper money had been the bane of the Confederation and the States. Madison raised the question whether it would not be enough to forbid that such bills be made a legal tender, that is, equivalent to gold or silver coin. He thought that would check the paper-money evil. Seventy-five years thereafter (February, 1862) the question stirred the country when Congress issued $150,000,000 of paper money known (because of the color) as "greenbacks," which were made "a legal tender in payment of all debts, public and private, within the United States." A woman who had before the passage of this Act become bound to pay a stated number of *dollars* in what was at that time the money of the United States tendered "greenbacks" (worth less than coin), which were refused. When the case reached the Suprene Court of the United States, Salmon P. Chase, who as Secretary of the Treasury in Lincoln's Cabinet had advocated the law, had been made Chief Justice. In an opinion written by him (upon fuller study, as he explained) the Act (and one of 1863) was held (1869) beyond the constitutional power of Congress, the chief ground being that the power of Congress could not be implied, and that the acts of Congress could not apply to debts contracted before their passage. Soon after the Greenback Case was decided, the Supreme Court was enlarged from seven judges to nine. In 1872 two similar cases were disposed of by the Court, one involving a debt contracted before the acts of Congress and one an obligation arising subsequently thereto. The Supreme Court overruled its

> decision in the first case and held that the war powers granted to Congress by the Constitution warranted the legislation.
>
> Next the question came up whether Congress could issue legal tender paper in time of peace, as well as in time of war. In 1878 it passed such an act. The other cases had been rested by the Supreme Court on the war power of Congress. It was believed by many that the Supreme Court could go no further. But in the Last Legal Tender Case (1884) it held that, whether in peace or war, when the exigency is so great, owing to "unusual and pressing demands on the resources of the government, or of the inadequacy of the supply of gold and silver," that it is expedient to resort to such means, the question of exigency is political and not judicial, and therefore to be determined, not by the courts, but by Congress. The Court said that "the power to make the notes of the Government a legal tender in payment of private debts" is "one of the powers belonging to sovereignty in other civilized nations."

In the preceding quotation it states that the Supreme Court decided that Congress had the power to declare the United States notes to be legal tender on the basis of exigency, expediency or sovereignty in other nations and not on any provision in the United States Constitution. We might ask the question, was that the intention of the writers of the Constitution?

In 1878, Congress authorized the issuance of silver certificates which were redeemable in silver dollars and later in silver bullion and declared them to be legal tender for all debts, public and private. After June 25, 1968, they were no longer redeemable and they no longer circulated as currency. They are still legal tender.

The Coinage Act of 1965 made the copper and nickel alloy fifty-cent, twenty-five cent and the ten-cent coins legal tender. It also made the United States notes legal tender even after the phrases "at its face value" and "Will Pay To The Bearer On Demand" were removed from the notes. Likewise, the same Coinage Act of 1965 made the Federal Reserve notes legal tender at the time the phrases "and is redeemable in Lawful Money at the United States Treasury, or at any Federal Reserve Bank" and "Will pay to the bearer on demand" were removed from the notes.

Thus we see that when government officials ignore the Constitution they may declare any currency to be legal tender. The result is that when a contract is written requiring that a future payment be made in legal tender, the parties to the contract have no sure way of knowing with what type of currency the future payment will be made, whether or not that legal tender will be available, or whether or not that future payment will be a just or an unjust settlement of the debt.

A careful study will teach us that if the items used as media of exchange have exchange value in themselves, or are redeemable for items with exchange value, or may be redeemed when they are presented as a payment for taxes, there will be no need for them to be declared to be legal tender.

Most of us wish to follow the Constitution, but to do so in this case we must first determine what the writers of the Constitution meant by the provision in Article I, Section 10 that stated "No State shall make any Thing but gold and silver coin a tender in Payment of debts."

Why did they word that statement in the negative? Was it because The Articles of Confederation gave the Continental Congress the right to issue bills of credit (if nine states assented) and declare them to be legal tender? Was it because they remembered the inflations of the currency that took place when bills of credit were declared to be legal tender?

In considering the question of whether or not the Constitution should give Congress the power to issue bills of credit, James Madison suggested that it might be all right provided Congress were not given the power to declare the bills of credit to be legal tender. After due deliberation the Constitution was finally written and Congress was not given either the power to issue bills of credit or the power to make anything a legal tender.

The negative wording in Article I, Section 10 suggests that the writers of the Constitution were not inclined to permit the states to have the right to declare anything to be legal tender, but reluctantly allowed them to declare gold and silver coins to be legal tender because the states were already doing that with the foreign gold and silver coins.

If the writers of the Constitution were hesitant in giving the states the right to declare only gold and silver coins to be legal tender, they surely did not intend to give Congress the right to declare anything other than gold and silver coins to be legal tender.

Given the power of the states to declare gold and silver coins to be legal tender at the market value of their metal content at the time they are used as payment and the hypothetical power of Congress to declare them to be legal tender at their face value, which is the market value of their metal content at the time Congress authorizes them to be minted (which Congress unwisely did in 1792), the probability of unequal legal tender values arises. Inequality and confusion could also occur if the states declared only gold and silver coins to be legal tender and the Congress declared copper and/or nickel coins and unredeemable notes to be legal tender. Valid contracts for future payments in legal tender might be difficult to write. It seems unlikely that the writers of the Constitution had such intentions.

While the United States Constitution does not give Congress the power to declare anything to be legal tender, Article 1, Section 8, gives Congress the power to lay and collect taxes. With that power goes the right to declare which items will be received as payment for those taxes.

Valid contracts for future payments could be written so that they would be payable in the coins or certificates that the government would receive as payment for taxes, customs, and other public dues and redeem when they are presented as payment for certain specific taxes. They need not be declared to be legal tender.

TO COIN

The verb "to coin" means to make coins. It does not mean to write or to print on paper notes or certificates. Documents such as United States notes, Federal Reserve notes and gold or silver certificates are written or printed on paper. They are not coined.

If the writers of the Constitution wanted the Congress to have power to print notes to circulate as currency they would have stated that fact with the following words: The Congress shall have the power to coin money and to emit Bills or Bills of credit.

TO ISSUE: TO EMIT

To issue means to put out, to distribute or to place into circulation. It does not mean to coin or to print. Coins may be issued after they are made. Notes and certificates may be issued after they are printed or written.

When it is said that the Congress should issue all the money the people need, what is probably meant is that the Congress should issue all the media of exchange the people need. However, if Congress adheres to the Constitution it cannot just issue any type of coins or pieces of paper and declare them to be lawful money.

In addition to following the Constitution, the members of Congress must practice honesty in their actions. It is clearly dishonest, for example, for Congress to make a coin with six cents worth of metal and then pass a law declaring the coin to be worth one dollar as a payment for debts. It is honest, however, for the Congress to use that same coin as a one-dollar payment for its needed goods and services, levy a tax for the amount of the payment, and later receive and redeem that coin when it is presented as a payment for one dollar's worth of those taxes.

In Article I, Section 8, clause 1, Congress is given the power to impose and collect taxes. Here, too, the

Congress must carry out its responsibility with honesty and in a manner that is the least burdensome to the taxpayers. The power to levy and collect taxes includes the power to decide when, how, and with what the taxes are to be paid. It would not be proper for Congress to require that taxes be paid with gold, if gold was not made available to the taxpayers for that purpose.

It is Article I, Section 8, clause 1 that gives Congress the power to lay and collect taxes and to issue Tax Credit Certificates as the medium the government uses to pay for its needed goods and services and the medium used by the public to pay taxes the government has levied.

CASH

The word "cash" is a technical term used by banks and other financial institutions to mean the dollar amount of any or all of the following items they have on hand: United States coins, United States notes, Federal Reserve notes, United States postal money orders, checks drawn on some banks, and government checks drawn on the treasury of the United States.

CURRENCY

The word "currency" is derived from the word "current." The word "current" has two meanings: (1) belonging to the present time (2) moving, running, or flowing as a current of water. It is proper to use the word "currency" to mean those items currently used or circulating as media of exchange. So when United States notes, United States coins, and Federal Reserve notes are held by a bank or other financial institution, they are called cash. When the same items are held by the people in general, they are called currency. (Note: The word "dollar" is not used as the name of any items called currency or cash.)

BACKING OF CURRENCY

It is frequently stated that currency must be backed by gold or silver. It has also been said that our currency is backed by the faith of the people, or by the wealth of the whole country.

Let us ask what "backing of currency" actually means. When the word "backing" is applied to an item of currency, the only logical meaning it can have is that the item is redeemable for, and thus backed by something of value. If a token coin, a certificate, or a note is backed by gold or silver, it is redeemable in gold or silver. If a postage stamp is redeemable in postal service, it is backed by postal service. If a tax credit certificate is redeemable when it is presented as a payment for taxes, it is backed by the amount of the taxes it pays.

So it is meaningless to say that currency is backed by the faith of the people or by the wealth of the people. If each item of the currency is not redeemable for some specific item, it is not backed by or redeemable for anything. While our present currency is used as a medium of exchange, that is, to purchase items of value, it is none the less not *backed* by anything.

EXCHANGE VALUE OF CURRENCY

A bona fide item which is used as currency has the exchange value of its own intrinsic worth, such as a full bodied coin; or it has the exchange value of the item for which it is the evidence of a claim, such as a gold certificate or a certificate of credit. In the case where the item of currency is received as a payment for taxes, such as a tax credit certificate, it has the exchange value for the dollar amount of the tax payment for which it is accepted.

An item which government officials have declared to be legal tender, such as a Federal Reserve note, has the *legal* exchange value of its face value for the payment of public and private debts.

But when government officials declare an item which otherwise has no exchange value to be legal tender, it may sometimes create great injustice. As previously noted, that is what took place in Germany between 1921 and 1923, when the German government officials declared the Reichsbank's notes (the equivalent of our Federal Reserve notes) to be legal tender. If a life insurance policy of 1000 marks matured in Germany in 1923, the 1000 marks would not buy a ten cent loaf of bread. Whereas five years earlier the 1000 marks were worth $250 in United States currency.

We occasionally hear or read that currency is the evidence of a claim for any goods or services being offered for sale. If a currency is the evidence of a claim, it is a document. A bona fide document will have written on it the item for which it is the evidence of a claim. If it is a claim for silver, that fact will be stated on the document as it was written on our silver certificates. But even when we had silver certificates, those certificates gave evidence of a claim only for silver. They did not give evidence of a claim for meat or potatoes or anything else.

There are continuing efforts to establish a currency that will have the same exchange value five, ten, or twenty years in the future that it now has. These efforts are futile because they are not based on reality.

A gold certificate only promised the bearer a specific amount of gold, nothing else. It did not promise that the bearer could claim (buy) the same amount of goods or services at some future time as he could when he earned the gold certificate.

Sometimes United States coins and notes, as well as Federal Reserve notes, are called tokens. They are tokens only in the sense that they do not have exchange value in themselves. They are not bona fide tokens because they are not redeemable in anything. A bona fide token is redeemable for the item for which it is the evidence of a claim.

Before 1933, it was proper to call fractional coins,

gold and silver certificates, United States notes, and even the Federal Reserve notes bona fide tokens because they were redeemable or exchangeable for gold.

Even though our currency is composed of non-bona fide tokens, it still has legal exchange value because our government officials have declared every item of it to be legal tender.

There is a difference between currency which is declared to be legal tender and is *receivable* as a payment for taxes and a bona fide tax credit certificate which is *redeemable* when it is used as a payment for taxes. The amount of redeemable tax credit certificates that can be issued is restricted to the amount of taxes levied. These certificates are self limiting and thus inflation of the currency cannot occur. A currency which is declared to be legal tender but is not redeemable in anything is not self limiting, so inflation can and does occur.

CURRENCY AS A STORE OF VALUE

Some textbooks teach that money (currency) serves as a store of value. Can an item which serves as a store of value simultaneously serve as currency?

The term "store of value" when applied to an item is intended to mean that the item will have approximately the same exchange value at some future time as it does at present.

In order for an item to serve as a store of exchange value it must have exchange value in itself or it must be the evidence of a claim for an item with exchange value. Full bodied coins could serve as a store of value because they have exchange value in themselves. Bona fide certificates of credit also could serve as a store of value up to the date of their redemption because they are the evidence of demand claims for goods or services which have exchange value.

If one wanted, however, to have full bodied coins or certificates of credit to serve as a store of value, one could not at the same time use them as media of exchange. Some people keep silver coins as a store of value, which means, of course, that the coins are not being used as a medium of exchange.

If a person deposits full bodied coins in a savings account in a bank, he no longer owns the coins. He bought a savings account deposit with his coins, which now belong to the bank. When the person wishes to withdraw the coins, the bank will give him whatever currency is then being used. It will buy back that account deposit with the currency then in circulation. This happens because one must accept whatever currency the government has declared to be legal tender. If the government were to stop declaring any currency to be legal tender, one could make an agreement with the bank to have his deposits returned with the same type of items he deposited.

Gold and silver coins will serve as a store of value only if they are actually stored in a home vault, warehouse or a safety deposit box.

A coin or a bill which the government has declared to be legal tender may serve as currency but one cannot be sure that it will serve as a store of exchange value. It may not have exchange value in itself and it may not be the evidence of a claim for goods or services with exchange value. So, if we wish to have something as a store of value, we must possess an item with exchange value or we must possess a bona fide claim for an item with exchange value.

DOLLARS ARE NOT CURRENCY

We should be aware of the difference between the meaning of the word "currency" and the meaning of the word "dollar." (An explanation of the meaning of the word "dollar" is given later in this chapter.) The word "currency" does not mean dollars. The exchange value of United States currency is expressed in the units called dollars. One does not have dollars in his pocket, but rather a number of dollars' worth of currency. When a person has fifty dollars' worth of coins or fifty dollars' worth of Federal Reserve notes, it is correct to say that he has fifty dollars' worth of currency.

ORDERS TO PAY CURRENCY

One person may order another person to pay currency to a third person. This is done by means of written orders called bills of exchange, checks, drafts, money orders and other written orders, or by direct verbal, telephone or telegraph orders.

AGREEMENTS TO PAY CURRENCY

When an agreement is made between a corporation and a bank for the bank to pay or transfer funds from the corporation's account to the accounts of others, such payments are made without using any actual items as checks or currency. Such a system of agreements and payments is called a moneyless, cashless, checkless money system.

If this system is done without inccuring interest bearing debts, it is harmless. But if it is carried out through the use of the fractional reserve banking system, ever increasing interest-bearing debts will be the result.

PROMISES TO REDEEM—WAREHOUSE RECEIPTS—CERTIFICATES OF CREDIT

Our former gold and silver certificates were redeemable for gold and silver held by the government. Because the certificates were redeemable for a specific number of grains of the metal, they could be called warehouse receipts.

Bona fide warehouse receipts and certificates of credit are redeemable for goods held by the issuer. Therefore, when they are brought into circulation and used as media of exchange, they do not create interest bearing debts or inflation.

PROMISES TO PAY CURRENCY—NOTES—BILLS OF CREDIT—BANK CREDIT

A person, bank, corporation, or governmental body promises to pay currency to another person at a specified time or when certain conditions are fulfilled. The means by which this is usually done are varied: They may be promises called notes, the signing of written applications for credit and credit cards, a bank officer's verbal promise to pay out currency for the demand deposit accounts he accepts, and the magic words, "charge it," spoken by a buyer with a good credit.

When notes, bills of credit, and bank credit are used as purchasing media, interest bearing debts are always incurred and an inflation of the purchasing media may follow, because they are promises to pay currency which the issuer does not yet possess.

When a bank or a governmental body can issue promises to pay what they do not have, there is no limit to the amount that can be issued. These are the notes, bills of credit, and bank credit that have not served well as purchasing media.

DOLLAR—THE NAME OF THE UNIT WE USE TO EXPRESS EXCHANGE VALUE; THE NAME OF OUR UNIT OF ACCOUNT

The word "dollar" at times was said to have meant a certain number of grains of silver or gold. The regular United States silver dollar coins have always contained 371.25 grains of pure silver.

When agreements were made that a payment was to be made in silver dollar coins, it was understood to mean that for each dollar payment due the creditor, he would receive a coin with 371.25 grains of silver. Sometimes the government or others would accept bullion in place of coins. It was agreed, in those cases, that 371.25 grains of silver bullion would be accepted as payment for each dollar due. So it was easy for government officials to declare that a dollar was 371.25 grains of silver. But declaring or calling 371.25 grains of silver a dollar did not make it the unit used to express exchange value. It only meant that 371.25 grains of silver was accepted as a payment for each dollar's debt.

As long as 371.25 grains of silver had a market value of one dollar, a debtor could give and a creditor would accept 371.25 grains of silver as a one dollar payment.

However, between 1878 and 1964 the market value of 371.25 grains of silver was less than one dollar. For many of those years 371.25 grains of silver was worth about 50 cents. If during those years 371.25 grains of silver could be given to pay a one dollar debt, a person could have bought 371.25 grains of silver for 50 cents and used it to pay off a one dollar debt. Of course that did not happen because a creditor would not accept it as a full payment.

On the other hand, when the market value of 371.25 grains of silver is above one dollar, as it has been since 1965, a debtor will not offer it for a one dollar payment. The above facts show that 371.25 grains of silver will not always serve as a dollar payment. The word "dollar" (not 371.25 grains of silver) is the name of the unit used to express the exchange value of a payment as well as the exchange value of goods, services, and currency. Thus, the unit called dollar is a common denominator unit used to express exchange value.

When the government issued silver certificates on which was written, "This certifies that there is on deposit in the treasury of the United States of America . . . dollars in silver payable to the bearer on demand," it was necessary for the government to declare the number of grains of silver that was on deposit for each dollar claimed by those certificates. Again it was easy to think that 371.25 grains of silver was a dollar.

When the word "dollar" is applied to a coin, the word is used as an adjective, not as a noun. It tells us that the coin is a one-dollar coin, not a half-dollar coin. When the word "dollar" is applied to a Federal Reserve note, it also is used as an adjective, not a noun. It tells us that the note is a one-dollar note, not a five or ten-dollar note.

So, if a coin collector will exchange his three one-dollar Federal Reserve notes for a one-dollar silver coin, he is not giving three dollars for one dollar; he is giving three (one-dollar Federal Reserve) notes for one (one-dollar) coin.

When the word "dollar" is correctly used as a noun, it is a descriptive term for a concept: The abstract unit we in the United States use to express our idea of the exchange value of one item in relation to the exchange value of one or more other items.

If we say a bushel of wheat is worth four dollars, we express our idea that a bushel of wheat can be exchanged for four dollars' worth of United States currency. If we then say that a bushel of oats is worth two dollars, we are expressing both the idea that a bushel of oats can be exchanged for two dollars' worth of U.S. currency, and that a bushel of wheat can be exchanged for two bushels of oats.

Because the abstract unit called "dollar" can be applied to all items with exchange value—property, goods, services, debts, taxes, expenditures, income, and United States currency—it is called a common denominator unit with which we express exchange value. It is the unit we use in accounting. It is called the unit of account.

When gold coins were used as currency, some agreements were made so that the debtor had to make his payments in dollars' worth of gold. The government also accepted gold at the mint for which it issued gold certificates. So it was necessary for the government to set a standard number of grains of gold for each dollar payment. That is why it was said that from 1792 to 1834 the dollar was 24.75 grains of pure gold; from 1834 to 1837 it was 23.20 grains; from 1837 to 1934 it was 23.22 grains; and from 1934 to 1971 it was 13.71 grains of gold for United States currency held outside of the United States.

Assertions by the government or anyone else that a

certain number of grains of gold were a dollar did not make it so; grains of gold could not logically be referred to by the same term used for the unit expressing exchange value.

If the government declares that a dollar payment means a payment of whatever number of grains of gold or silver it may decide upon and if it can change that number of grains of gold or silver whenever it wants to (as it has done in the past), people who write contracts for future payments to be made in dollars will not know for certain the number of grains of gold or silver that the government might require for each future dollar payment. They will not know if the future payment will be a just payment.

When the government bought or sold (made exchanges of) gold at $1 for 13.71 grains (1/35 ounce), it meant the government had a fixed buying and selling price on the gold; and that is all it meant.

When the word "dollar" is used as the name of the *unit* with which we express the exchange value of a coin, the word "dollar" does not mean the coin; and it does not mean a certain number of grains of the metal in the coin. It is the name of the unit people in the United States adopted as a common denominator unit with which to express the exchange value of property, goods, services, debts, taxes, expenditures, income, and United States currency. It is our unit of account.

CHECK

A check is a written order to a bank to pay currency (coins or notes) to a specific payee or to the bearer on demand. Thus a check is not currency and it is not the actual payment.

When a person buys an item, let us say for $100, and gives the seller his check for $100 for the item, he does not pay for the item with the check. The seller accepts the check for the item but he has not yet been paid. The check is an order to the bank to pay $100 worth of currency to the seller. It is the bank that must pay the currency to the seller when the check is presented for payment.

If the check were the payment, the seller would be paid twice, once with the check and again with the currency. A check is like a doctor's prescription. The prescription is not the medicine. It is an order to the druggist to make or prepare the medicine. Likewise, a check is an order by the drawer of the check to the bank to give the payee a specific amount of currency.

A cashier's check is an order written by an authorized officer of a bank ordering his own bank to pay currency to a specific payee.

A bank draft is an order written by an authorized officer of a bank ordering another bank to pay currency to a specific payee.

INFLATION

The word "inflation" used by itself often confuses people because there are different interpretations of its meaning. Similarly, the term "inflation of the currency" is not always clear. An inflation of the currency only means an increase of United States coins, United States notes, and Federal Reserve notes. The expression, "inflation of the purchasing media" (currency and bank credit), is the appropriate term to use in discussing inflation. Even in using that term, however, we must make it clear that we do not mean the normal and proper increase of the purchasing media in circulation which is at a rate not greater than the rate of increase of the amount of goods and services being offered for sale.

To maintain stable prices and normal production the amount of purchasing media in circulation must be increased or decreased at the same rate as the rate of increase or decrease of the goods and services being offered for sale.

We conclude, therefore, that when the word "inflation" or the term "inflation of the purchasing media" is used, it should mean the situation that exists when the purchasing media is placed in circulation at a faster or greater rate than the rate of increase of the goods and services being offered for sale. The effect of that situation will be an increase of the general price level.*

FULL BODIED COINS

When the market value of the metal in a coin and the legal tender value of the coin are equal, the coin is called a full bodied coin.

TOKEN COINS

When the market value of the metal in a coin is less than the legal tender value of the coin, it is called a token coin.

NON-CIRCULATING COINS

When the market value of the metal in a coin is greater than the legal tender value of the coin, the coin will no longer circulate as a medium of exchange. It will be kept as a store of value or exchanged at its higher market value.

CHAPTER II

QUALITIES OF THE ITEMS THAT SERVE AS MEDIA OF EXCHANGE

Experience has taught us that when we use as media of exchange coins, notes, certificates, bills, and demand deposits with undesirable qualities, the people are burdened, at times, with deflations, inflations, general

---

*For a more detailed discussion of inflation, see Popp, *Money: Bona Fide or Non-Bona Fide*, Ch. XII.

unemployment, poverty, and always with economic uncertainty and ever increasing interest-bearing debts.

We know that there are a number of different items that can serve as media of exchange. We know that some of these items are brought into circulation by a governmental body and some by private corporations. We know that some are paid into circulation, some are loaned into circulation and some are sold into circulation.

When a governmental body borrows the media of exchange it needs from private corporations, such as banks, it incurs interest-bearing debts whether the media borrowed are coins, notes, certificates, or bank credit. Such a governmental body is not a sovereign body. A sovereign governmental body does not have to borrow from anyone.

Also, when private corporations and individuals who produce and distribute goods and services depend only upon governmental bodies for the media of exchange they need, they are not a free people. Their economic activities are controlled by the actions and the lack of actions of government officials.

Likewise, when most of the media of exchange in a country is bank credit loaned into circulation to governmental bodies and to the private producers and distributors of goods and services, the governmental bodies and the producers and distributors of goods and services are both dependent upon the good will of the issuers of the bank credit. Both are not free. They cannot operate unless they incur an interest-bearing debt. If they do not incur an interest-bearing debt, they will not have the media of exchange they need to operate. That is the situation in most countries of the world today, including the United States.

When the items which can serve as media of exchange, such as our present coins and our former silver certificates, are sold into circulation, no interest-bearing debt occurs; but that method cannot be used in a country where no other media of exchange exists with which to buy such items.

When coins, notes, or certificates are redeemable for goods or services or as payment for taxes, no inflation of the media of exchange will occur and no governmental body or Federal Reserve System is needed to control the amount issued.

When those who issue the media of exchange do so in good faith, no one will obtain an unearned gain and no one will incur an un-deserved loss from such issues.

The following are the desirable qualities in the items that serve as media of exchange:

1. They are to be paid into circulation.
2. They are to be redeemable for goods or services or as payment for taxes.
3. When demand deposits are used as media of exchange, they are to have 100% cash reserves on deposit in the bank.
4. All are to be issued in good faith.

Let us now point out the desirable and the undesirable qualities of several items that now serve or have served in the past as media of exchange.

UNITED STATES FULL BODIED GOLD AND SILVER COINS

Their desirable qualities were that they were paid into circulation. No interest-bearing debt was incurred. They did not have to be redeemed for anything because they had full exchange value in themselves.

The one undesirable quality the full bodied gold and silver coins had was that Congress placed a fixed exchange value, a legal tender value, on the coins at the time they were minted. That is why they did not stay in circulation.

The coins would have stayed in circulation if the Congress would have declared the legal tender value to be equal to the market value of the metal content of the coins at the times the coins were received by the government as a payment or paid out by the government as a payment. That was what the writers of the Constitution meant for Congress to do when they stated, "Congress shall have the power to regulate the value thereof."

UNITED STATES TOKEN COINS NOW IN CIRCULATION

One very desirable quality of our token coins is that they are sold into circulation without incurring an interest-bearing debt.

They have three undesirable qualities:

1. They are not redeemable for anything.
2. They are sold at the same price they would be if they were full bodied coins; which they are not.
3. They are issued in denominations suitable only to make small payments.

If they were issued in large as well as small denominations, paid into circulation, and redeemed when presented as payment for a specific tax, they would have all the desirable qualities needed to serve well as media of exchange.

SILVER CERTIFICATES ISSUED BY THE UNITED STATES GOVERNMENT

The silver certificates had one desirable quality, that is, they were sold into circulation without incurring an interest-bearing debt.

Another quality they had was that each dollar's worth of the certificates could be redeemed for 371.25 grains of silver. Note: That each dollar's worth of the certificates was not redeemable for one dollar's worth of silver, even though it seemed to say so on the certificates.

These silver certificates were warehouse receipts for 371.25 grains of silver for each dollar's worth of the certificates. They also were certificates of legal tender. These two facts were written on each certificate. That meant the certificates had two exchange values: One the legal tender value, the other the market value of 371.25 grains of silver for each dollar's worth of the certificates.

When the price of silver was less than one dollar for 371.25 grains, they served as a medium of exchange because they were certificates of legal tender. When the market value of 371.25 grains of silver went above one dollar, they were not used as media of exchange. They were used only as warehouse receipts.

UNITED STATES NOTES

These notes were issued by the United States government only in the years of 1862 and 1863. They had two desirable qualities: They were paid into circulation and they did not incur an interest-bearing debt.

The undesirable feature of these notes is that they were not redeemable in anything. It is true that they contained a promise to pay dollars (in coin) on demand, but the government did not have any dollar's worth of coins with which to pay the notes and it did not, at that time, make any provision to obtain any.

It might have been more appropriate to call these notes certificates of legal tender for all debts, except for the payment of custom duties and interest on the public debt. Because that is what they really were at the time they were issued. That statement was written on each note.

If the United States notes would have been issued as bona fide tax credit certificates, they would have had all the desirable qualities needed to serve very well as media of exchange.

FEDERAL RESERVE NOTES

The current Federal Reserve notes have no desirable qualities.

They have a number of undesirable qualities. They are loaned into circulation. An interest-bearing debt is incurred to bring them into circulation. They are not redeemable for anything. They are not bona fide notes. A note is the written evidence of a promise to pay. The current Federal Reserve notes give no such evidence.

The Federal Reserve Banks obtain the notes from the government for the cost of the paper and printing. At the present time the cost is about one cent per note.

If a local bank should wish to obtain any of the notes, it must give the Federal Reserve Bank an interest-bearing government bond equal in value to the value of the notes it receives. The Federal Reserve Bank will receive the interest on that bond. In effect it receives interest on the notes it obtained for the cost of the paper and printing.

We said the Federal Reserve notes are not notes. Then, what are they? They are certificates of legal tender signed by the treasurer and the secretary of the treasury of the United States. They are not signed by any official of a Federal Reserve Bank.

There is no need for the United States government to give the notes to the Federal Reserve Banks. If the government desires to issue certificates of legal tender, it could issue them as such and pay them into circulation and no interest-bearing bond would be needed to bring them into circulation.

DEMAND DEPOSITS OF CASH

When a person deposits cash and/or its equivalent in checks in his checking account, those deposits have the desirable qualities needed to serve as media of exchange. They are paid into circulation. No interest-bearing debt occurs. They are redeemable for cash. The bank can pay them out in good faith because it receives 100% cash for reserves for those deposits.

Demand deposits with 100% cash reserves have no undesirable qualities when used as media of exchange.

DEMAND DEPOSITS OF BANK CREDIT

Demand deposits of bank credit have none of the

desirable qualities needed for a medium of exchange. They are loaned into circulation. They incur an interest-bearing debt. They do not have 100% cash reserves on deposit in the bank. They are not notes; they are not certificates; they are not metal tokens; they are not physical things. They exist in the form of bookkeeping entries of credits and debits.

They come into existence when they are entered as a bookkeeping credit in a borrower's demand deposit account. They are transferred from one person or entity to another person or entity by written orders (checks) and sometimes by verbal orders.

When demand deposits of bank credit are loaned out for any purpose other than to bring goods to market, an inflation of the general price level can occur.

The use of demand deposits of bank credit as media of exchange is the reason why we have at times inflations and deflations of the purchasing media and always ever increasing government and private interest-bearing debts.

TAX CREDIT CERTIFICATES

Tax credit certificates are certificates issued by a governmental body in lieu of issuing interest-bearing bonds. They may be issued in the form of coins and/or certificates. They may be issued in large and small denominations.

They have all the desirable qualities needed to serve as good media of exchange. Their issuance does not cause an interest-bearing debt. They are paid into circulation in exchange for the goods and services received by the governmental body. At tax-paying time they are received and redeemed as payment for the taxes levied at the time they were issued.

Because they are receivable as payment for all customs, fees, fines, and other charges due the government, people will use them as media of exchange from the time they are paid out until they are used as payment for the taxes for which they are redeemed.

The fact that a tax is levied in an amount equal to the amount of the certificates issued tells us that they are issued in good faith.

The government of England issued tax credit certificates in the form of tally sticks from the year 1100 to the year 1694 A.D. without incurring interest-bearing debts.

Tax credit certificates could also be called tax payment certificates.

CERTIFICATES OF CREDIT

Certificates of credit, frequently called gift certificates, are issued by producers and distributors of goods and services. They have the desirable qualities required of a good medium of exchange.

They are either paid or sold into circulation without incurring an interest-bearing debt. They are redeemable for the goods or services the issuer is offering for sale. They are issued in good faith because the issuer can only honestly issue them as the evidence of a claim for the goods or services he has available.

They can be issued in the form of metal tokens or in the form of certificates. They can be issued in large and/or small denominations.

Utility companies and other corporations that borrow funds could issue them in lieu of borrowing and use them as payment for a part of the goods and services they receive. From the time they are paid out until they are redeemed people could use them as media of exchange. For every dollar's worth of certificates issued and paid out, the issuer would have one less dollar's worth of interest-bearing debts.

DEBT MONEY SYSTEM VERSUS CREDIT MONEY SYSTEM

When we use, as we are now using, items to serve as media of exchange which are brought into circulation by incurring interest-bearing debts, we have a *debt money system*.

Whereas, if tax credit certificates and/or certificates of credit were used as media of exchange, we would have a *credit money system*. No interest-bearing debts would be incurred.

The debt money system gives us inflations and deflations, booms and busts, bank failures, bankruptcies, balances of payments deficits and surpluses, future economic uncertainties, and ever increasing interest-bearing debts.

A credit money system would not cause any of these problems because no interest-bearing debts would be incurred and yet we could have all the media of exchange we would need.

CHAPTER III

GRESHAM'S LAW

We learn from history that in 1558 a certain Sir Thomas Gresham gave Queen Elizabeth a maxim about money. Various writers have different versions of what he is supposed to have said. The following are examples:

1. Bad money drives good money out of circulation.
2. Inferior money tends to drive preferred money out of circulation.
3. A less valuable money will drive a more valuable money out of circulation.

It is not important for us to know precisely what Sir Thomas Gresham said to Queen Elizabeth. But it is important that we understand why some money ceased to be used as currency.

If we use the word "coin" in place of the word "money," we may more easily understand what was meant because the word "money" meant coins to Sir Thomas, to Queen Elizabeth, and to almost everyone else until recent times. Terms such as "good" and "bad" when applied to coins are inappropriate. Coins are neither good nor bad. Some coins may have less exchange value than others, but that does not make them bad.

One coin will not and cannot drive another coin out of circulation. People will simply exchange their coins for the highest value they can get. People will use a coin as a medium of exchange so long as its exchange value for any other purpose is less than the government-set exchange value as legal tender or as a payment for taxes. No other coin will drive it out of circulation.

For example, if the price of copper should increase to $1.50 per pound, people would quickly sell (exchange) their copper coins because it takes only 147 cents to make a pound. The one-cent coins would no longer be used as currency but not because they were driven out of circulation by other coins. People would simply exchange them for a value which is higher than the government-set legal tender value.

If Sir Thomas Gresham had done his homework, he would have told Queen Elizabeth that when a coin is given a fixed legal tender value, it means that the coin has two exchange values. It has the market exchange value of the metal it contains and it has the legal tender exchange value set by the government; and people can be expected to exchange the coin for whichever value is higher. As long as its set legal tender value is higher than its exchange value for any other purpose, it will circulate as a currency. Its exchange value for any other purpose may drop to zero, but it will continue to circulate as a medium of exchange.

If at any time, however, the market exchange value of the metal in the coin became greater than the set legal tender value of the coin, the coin would no longer be used as currency. It would be hoarded or exchanged for the higher value. Thus, we can conclude the people will not use coins as currency if and when they have an exchange value for other purposes which is higher than their set value as legal tender.

We may conclude, too, that when a government sets a legal tender value on a coin, or on any other item used as a medium of exchange, it must set that legal tender value higher than, or at least equal to, its exchange value for any other purpose. Otherwise people will use such item for purposes other than a medium of exchange.

It makes no sense for a government to place a legal tender value on gold or silver coins, if that legal tender value is higher or lower than the market value of the metal in the coins. If the legal tender value of the coins is higher than their exchange value as a commodity, then the coins need not be gold or silver. A cheaper metal would serve the same purpose. If the legal tender value of the coins is less than their exchange value as a commodity, the coins will be hoarded or exchanged for their higher value as a commodity. They will not be used as legal tender.

Gold and silver coins (900 fine) could be useful, though not necessary, as media of exchange so long as the government did not give them a set legal tender value or a fixed price at the time they were minted. People will determine for themselves the exchange value of the coins at the time of each transaction. That is what coin dealers and collectors do now. They have no need for the government to set an exchange value on the coins. The government should set the legal tender value, the market value, on the coins only when they are presented as payment to the government and when the government uses them as payment to others.

It is not only coins that cease to circulate as currency because of Gresham's Law. When paper currency has more than one exchange value, people will also exchange it for its highest value. For example, when we had silver certificates, the silver certificates had two exchange values:

1. The government declared them to be legal tender at their face value.
2. The government promised to redeem them at the

rate of 371.25 grains of silver for each dollar's worth of silver certificates.

For many years (from 1878 to 1964) the 371.25 grains of silver was worth less than one dollar, and at times it was worth less than fifty cents; the legal tender value, however, always remained at the face value of one dollar. The result was that the certificates were used as currency for those many years. People did not redeem the certificates for silver until the price of the 371.25 grains of silver was worth more than one dollar's worth of other currency. Then the silver certificates were no longer used as legal tender or as currency. It was not other coins or currency that drove the certificates out of circulation; people merely exchanged them for an item (silver) which had an exchange value that was greater than the legal tender value or face value of the certificates.

Perhaps an appropriate definition for Gresham's Law may be stated as follows: When an item which is used as currency acquires an exchange value that is greater than its government-set exchange value as legal tender, it will no longer be offered as legal tender or as a medium of exchange.

CHAPTER IV

STANDARD OF VALUE

Some textbooks use the term "standard of value" as one of the qualities or functions of money (currency). It is stated that currency (money) is the standard which people use to measure the value of goods and services.

Let us examine that idea in order to determine

whether or not people really use the items of the currency to measure exchange value.

First, instead of the word "value" it is more accurate to use the term "exchange value." There are a number of values which may be applied to goods and services. When we say that an item has exchange value we mean that the item has certain desirable qualities for which others will be willing to give goods or services of their own.

We must now ask, is there any government-set standard by which the giver and the receiver of an item can determine how much of one item must be given or taken in exchange for the other item? If the answer is yes, then it is clear that we have an established standard of exchange values to which we must conform.

While it is true that the government has established certain standards for coins and for a number of other items, such as weights and measurements, it has not established standards to which we must conform our idea of the exchange values of goods and services.

The government only establishes exchange value standards to which we must conform when it freezes or controls wages and prices. That system works moderately well only if the government continually adjusts the wages and the prices to correspond to the normal market prices which would prevail if there were no such controls.

The government has established a unit, called the dollar, with which we can express our idea of the exchange value of any goods or services. But the dollar unit is not a standard that we use to determine or measure the amount of exchange value of goods and services.

We know that the unit we use to express the weight of objects, the pound, is not the standard metal block kept at the Bureau of Standards. The weight of that block of metal is expressed with the concept unit called the pound. The word "pound" is the name of the unit used to express, not measure, the weight of that certain standard block of metal. The block of metal and the unit used to express its weight are two different things. The weight of an object is measured by the use of a scale and then the amount of the weight is expressed in the units called pounds.

Although the government has not officially established standards for determining the exchange value of goods and services, there are standards which one may choose for the purpose of determining the exchange value of an item he is appraising. Every appraiser compares the item he is appraising with other items, the exchange value of which he knows. Those other items are the standards he uses for the purpose of determining the exchange value of the item he is appraising.

Currency is an item with exchange value. So when a person gives or takes currency in a transaction he first appraises the exchange value of the currency, comparing it with the item having the highest exchange value for which it may be traded. That item will be the standard that he will use to determine the amount of the exchange value of the currency. For example, between 1934 and August 15, 1971, residents of foreign countries were promised by the government of the United States that each dollar's worth of U.S. currency they held could be exchanged for 1/35 ounce of gold. That was one of the standards these individuals could use at that time. They also were promised that U.S. currency could be exchanged for goods and services in the United States at the same exchange value as the currency held by the residents of the United States. That was another standard for them.

On August 15, 1971, the promise of the United States to exchange gold for foreign held United States currency was rescinded. After August 15, 1971, the items for which they could exchange U.S. currency were our goods and services. The amount of our goods and services that they could obtain for each dollar's worth of U.S. currency then became the most important standard for them to use to determine the exchange value of foreign held U.S. currency.

transactions. No one, not even government officials, can succeed in setting the market value of anything, including full bodied coins, for a future time.

CHAPTER VI

A UNIT USED TO EXPRESS EXCHANGE VALUE: A UNIT OF ACCOUNT

Before people used coins or currency as media of exchange, they traded their goods and services by direct barter. A man might exchange one cow for five small pigs, one pig for ten chickens, one day's labor for a bushel of potatoes, and so on. The exchange value of each item was expressed in the quantity and quality of the other items for which it could be exchanged.

There was no common denominator unit with which to express exchange value. There was no unit of account.

Let us try to give an explanation of how the unit of account was established by telling the story of Peter Meyer and Count Schlick. The story is in part true and in part fiction. Count Schlick is real. He lived and owned a silver mine in Bohemia. Peter Meyer is a fictitious character. The purpose of the story is to bring out the following important points:

1. How a common denominator unit of account was established.
2. The name given to that unit of account.
3. The purpose and function of the unit of account.
4. How the issuance of certificates of credit was made possible by the use of the unit of account.
5. How the certificates of credit were then used as a medium of exchange.
6. How these bona fide certificates of credit, which served as a medium of exchange, were brought into circulation:

   a. Without being issued by a governmental body or a bank.
   b. Without incurring interest bearing debts.
   c. Without anyone controlling the amount to be issued.
   d. Without causing an inflation of the money supply.

7. The origin of the word "dollar."
8. The origin of the first silver dollar coin.
9. The consequences resulting when a fixed exchange value is placed on precious metal coins.
10. The consequences resulting when the media of exchange are issued by a monopoly.
11. That, if any person or body of persons controls the supply of the items which serve as media of exchange, that person or body controls the price of all goods and services bought and sold with those items.
12. How the stealing and dishonest use of the items that serve as media of exchange could be reduced to a minimum.

IT HAPPENED IN BOHEMIA

Beginning in the year 1510 A.D. and for many years thereafter, a man whom we shall call Peter Meyer operated a large trading center (a general store) in St. Joachimsthal (St. Jochim's Dale), Bohemia.

People would bring to him items which they produced in order to exchange (barter) them for other goods which they wanted. These other items were produced by people who brought them to Peter Meyer also for the purpose of exchanging them for other things they wanted. Peter Meyer was the middle man.

In time, Peter Meyer acquired a large stock of goods. All transactions took place by negotiation which resulted in agreement, or direct barter. No coins or currency were used. The exchange value of each item was expressed in terms of the other items for which it could be traded. For example, one cow was worth five pigs, or five pigs were worth one cow. Neither party was a buyer or a seller. Both parties merely exchanged goods.

Although the exchange value of each item was set by agreement at the time an exchange took place, a generally understood ratio of exchange values did exist between the various items. It was generally understood that one pair of men's shoes was worth two men's shirts, or three bushels of wheat, or six bushels of potatoes, or 200 pounds of salt, or 50 pounds of sugar, or 12 pounds of butter, or 24 dozen eggs, and so on. Some adjustments were made because of supply and demand and the quality of the goods. For example, in the winter months a farmer would exchange only 12 dozen eggs for one pair of shoes, whereas in the summer he might exchange 24 dozen eggs for one pair of shoes.

This system worked fairly well for those transactions that were completed at one time. It did not work so well when the exchange was completed at a later date. Take the case of the shoemaker who wanted to receive his eggs over a period of time in exchange for a pair of shoes. The eggs were scarce in the winter. Sometimes none were available. There was no established way to predetermine the number of eggs the shoemaker could receive at a furture date for a pair of shoes. Other items, too, sometimes became scarce, so most transactions had to be completed at one time even though sometimes the people did not really want the items they had to take.

After some thought, Peter Meyer said to himself, there ought to be a common denominator unit with which I could express the exchange value of all items to be exchanged.

Suppose I use the exchange value of a bushel of wheat as a common denominator unit with which to express the exchange value of all items in my store; how would it work? Could I say, for example, that a bushel of potatoes has the exchange value of half a bushel of wheat, a pound of butter has the exchange value of one quarter bushel of wheat, a man's shirt has the exchange value of one bushel of wheat, a barrel of salt has the exchange value of two bushels of wheat, and so on?

I believe I could express the exchange value of everything in relation to the exchange value of a bushel of wheat. But wait a minute! How would I express the exchange value of a bushel of wheat? If I said a bushel of wheat has the exchange value of a bushel of wheat, that would be no different than saying that a pound of butter has the exchange value of a pound of butter. Or if I said that the exchange value of a bushel of wheat has the exchange value of a man's shirt, then the exchange value of a bushel of wheat would no longer be the common denominator unit. The exchange value of a man's shirt might become the common denominator unit. But we must have only one common denominator unit.

I must also consider that if, in a certain year, the crop of wheat is very small the exchange value of each bushel of wheat would be much greater than when the crop is normal.

Or if, in a certain year, the crop of wheat is much larger than normal the exchange value of each bushel of wheat would be less than when the crop is normal.

The result would be that the exchange value of the common denominator unit would increase or decrease according to the size of the crop of wheat. The result would be that I would be compelled to raise or lower the price (the expressed exchange value) of all goods other than wheat, according to the supply of wheat being offered for sale. Or I would be compelled to change the expressed exchange value of the common denominator unit, that is, a bushel of wheat. Such a system would not give me the stability in prices that I would like.

Therefore, I do not wish to adopt the exchange value of a commodity as the common denominator unit with which to express exchange values. First, because it does not provide the means to express the exchange value of itself, and second, when its own exchange value changes I will be compelled to change the prices of all other items.

But Peter Meyer kept thinking that there must be a way. So, one Sunday afternoon when Peter Meyer was supposed to be resting, he conceived another idea. He again said to himself, I shall adopt points as units with which to express the exchange value of my goods. I shall do the same for the items brought to me for trade. I shall apply the points so as to keep the same ratio of exchange values between the various items as I have been doing. If a pair of shoes has the exchange value of two shirts, it will be given two times the number of points as a shirt. And all items will be given points in the proper ratio with their exchange value in relation to the exchange value of the other items. I shall thus establish a system to express an accurate exchange value for every item. If the supply of an item becomes abundant, I can decrease the number of points applied to it without making any changes for the other items. If an item becomes scarce, I can increase the number of points applied to it. In that way, I shall be able to express the proper ratio of exchange value of each item as it relates to the exchange values of other items.

So, the next day Peter Meyer placed a "points" tag, a price tag, on all of his goods. The following are examples:

1 pair of men's shoes	6 points
1 men's shirt	3 points
1 bushel of wheat	2 points
100 pounds of salt	2 points
1 bushel of potatoes	1 point
8 pounds of sugar	1 point
1 pound of butter	1/2 point
1 dozen of eggs	1/4 point

These points were not monetary units. That is, they were not units of coins because no coins were used at that time by Peter Meyer or his customers. These points were abstract units. They were concepts used as units without exchange value in themselves. But when the units were applied to items by Peter Meyer, they expressed his idea of the exchange value that each item had in relation to the exchange value of every other item.

They were used as numbers are used. A number is an abstract quantity by itself. It must be applied to objects before it has meaning. The number ten means nothing by itself. But when we say ten boys or ten days, the number ten has a definite meaning.

If the point had no exchange value in itself, then what did it express? It expressed Peter Meyer's idea of the exchange value of each item in relation to the exchange value of each other item.

For example, if two points were applied to a bushel of wheat and six points were applied to a pair of shoes, it meant that Peter Meyer would exchange one pair of shoes for three bushels of wheat. A wheat grower, a shoemaker, or any other producer of goods could look at the point tags on the various items in Peter Meyer's store and determine how much of his product he would have to give in exchange for the items he wanted. In other words, the unit called "point" served the same purpose at that time as the unit called "dollar" serves now.

After Peter Meyer's customers became acquainted with the new system, they saw that they were making their exchanges for the same items in about the same ratio as they did before. They found that they now were negotiating the number of points applied to the items instead of the items themselves.

They also found that when they brought to Peter Meyer more points' worth of goods than the points' worth of goods they needed from him at that time, it was convenient for Peter Meyer to issue them a certificate of credit (a gift certificate) with which they could claim these extra points' worth of goods at a later time. The certificate of credit was a document that gave evidence of a claim for any of Peter Meyer's goods. This was a definite convenience which did not exist before the point system was adopted. The certificates of credit were issued in different denominations, such as one point, five points, ten points, twenty points, and in fractions of a point. For the fractions of a point, Peter Meyer adopted the decimal system. That is, he divided the point into 100 parts. Each part was called a centesimal point. Later, that was abbreviated to a centum point and, finally, it was simply called a cent.

Note: The cent was not the name of a coin. It was the name of the unit used to express the exchange value of an item in the amount of 1/100 parts of a point.

The following are sample copies of some of his certificates of credit:

10 Certificate of Credit 10

by

PETER MEYER

No.______ Date______

Within one year after date of issue, this Certificate will be accepted in exchange for

TEN POINTS'

worth of any goods being offered for exchange at

PETER MEYER'S EXCHANGE CENTER

(Signed by)__________

Peter Meyer

For

10 TEN POINTS 10

10/100 10/100

Certificate of Credit
by
PETER MEYER

No.______ Date______

Within one year after date of issue, this
Certificate will be accepted in exchange for

TEN CENTESIMAL POINTS'
worth of any goods being offered for exchange at

PETER MEYER'S EXCHANGE CENTER

(Signed by)__________
Peter Meyer

For
10/100 TEN CENTESIMAL POINTS 10/100

1/100 1/100

CERTIFICATE OF CREDIT
by
Peter Meyer

No.______ Date______

Within one year after date of issue, this
Certificate will be accepted in exchange for

ONE CENT'S

worth of any goods being offered for exchange at

PETER MEYER'S EXCHANGE CENTER

(Signed by)__________
Peter Meyer

For
1/100 ONE CENT 1/100

For identification purposes and to prevent loss from forgery and theft, Peter Meyer would keep a record of each certificate issued and each person who received the certificate could keep a record of the number on the face of the certificate and also write his name or identification mark on the back of the certificate. See the following sample:

Received by: Date ________

Because each owner could be required to identify himself, no one would be apt to forge or steal the certificate. And if the certificate were lost or destroyed, it would never be returned to Peter Meyer for redemption. So, after the redemption date passed, Peter Meyer could reimburse the owner in a manner that was mutually agreeable.

These certificates of credit were bona fide documents giving evidence of a claim for a specific number of exchange value units' (points') worth of goods held for exchange by Peter Meyer. They were not coins. They were not money. They were not issued by the government. They were not issued by a bank. Peter Meyer had the right to issue them because he possessed the goods for which they were the evidence of a claim. Peter Meyer did not have to borrow them. No interest was paid for their use.

However, they were negotiable and served as the medium of exchange. They had the exchange value of the amount of goods for which they were the evidence of a claim.

THE POINT BECAME THE UNIT OF ACCOUNT

Peter Meyer also learned that he could take an inventory of the exchange value of all his goods. He could keep an account of each day's business. Thus, the point was established as the unit of account. We see from this that the unit used to express exchange value was also the unit of account.

> (Buying and selling is the exchanging (bartering) of goods and services with the use of a medium of exchange. Exchanges are made conveniently when it is easy for those making the exchanges to obtain the necessary media of exchange.
>
> By paying for the goods with certificates of credit, Peter Meyer was, in effect, selling the equivalent amount of his other goods. All he had to do was just

keep the items until they were called for. The fact that it was easy for Peter Meyer to buy with the use of certificates made it easier for the producers of goods to sell their products to him.)

This system of using points as the units of accounting and as the units to express exchange value (the price), with certificates of credit for currency, worked very well. People could express the exchange value of goods and services in a fairly accurate manner. They could keep an account of the exchange value of all goods and services being traded. People could exchange (sell) their goods or services at one time and buy other items at a later time.

There was no shortage of currency because if a person had a surplus of wanted products, he could easily exchange them for Peter Meyer's certificates of credit. And those certificates of credit were accepted as bona fide currency because they were redeemable at Peter Meyer's Trading Center.

It was easy for Peter Meyer to pay for the goods he bought because he did not have to borrow or pay interest or go into debt to obtain the currency. After he paid out the certificates of credit, they would circulate as media of exchange until someone returned them to him for redemption.

When Peter Meyer received the goods, he issued his certificates of credit as payment. Those certificates were bona fide evidence that the bearer had a demand claim for the equivalent amount of any goods held in his store.

Note: There was no opportunity for anyone to cause an inflation of the currency because no inflationary certificates were issued. Every certificate was redeemable on demand. Peter Meyer had the goods on hand at the time he issued the certificates.

AND THEN A SILVER COIN WAS MADE

At the same time in the same village of St. Joachimsthal, a count by the name of Schlick was operating a silver mine and a silversmith shop. His mine at that time was the largest and the most productive silver mine in Europe. He sold silver products to silver buyers even in neighboring countries. He made various articles out of silver, such as silver platters, silver cups, and silverware. But, he still had a surplus of silver. So, in 1519 he made a large silver coin which bore the image of St. Joachim.

St. Joachimsthal was the name of the village and the large silver coin was given the name of the village. Each coin was called a St. Joachimsthaler, just as each automobile made by Henry Ford was called a Ford.

Because St. Joachimsthaler was a long name, people began to call the coin a thaler. In some German speaking areas it was called a taler. At that time the word "thaler" was not the name of the common denominator unit to express exchange value. It was not the name of the unit of account. It was only the name of a coin. At that time the word "point" was the name of the common denominator unit used to express exchange value and it was the name of the unit of account.

If we fully understand that there is a difference between a coin and a common denominator unit used to express the exchange value of goods, services, and coins, we will not be confused when later the word "thaler" or "dollar" is used to mean either a coin or a common denominator unit used to express exchange value.

A large number of these thalers were made and were used in the German speaking countries. Similar coins with similar names were made in other countries. In Denmark the name of the coin was *daler*, in Holland, *dalder*, in Italy, *tallero*, in Poland, *talar*, and in Spain, *dollar*.

All of these names were derivations of Joachimsthaler. In 1873 Germany replaced the thaler or taler with the mark as the name of its coin or monetary unit. The mark at that time was equivalent to half a thaler.

Count Schlick offered to exchange his newly made thalers for food, tools, and supplies at Peter Meyer's

Trading Center. After some negotiating, they agreed that each thaler would be exchanged for one point's worth of Peter Meyer's goods. That meant that each coin had an exchange value of one point's worth of Peter Meyer's goods.

Count Schlick was happy with the arrangement. He could, with the thalers he produced, obtain the supplies he needed for his family, his mine, his silversmith shop, and also pay the wages of his employees. His employees could exchange their earned thalers for the goods they needed at Peter Meyer's Trading Center. They knew that they could obtain one point's worth of goods for each thaler.

THE THALER COIN BECOMES A CERTIFICATE OF CREDIT

For some time Peter Meyer stored and exchanged these thalers as he did the other items he stocked. He and others considered the thalers only standarized pieces of silver, which were worth whatever their silver content was worth.

Count Schlick was producing a large quantity of the thalers. So many were brought to Peter Meyer that he became overstocked. He decided that he could solve the problem by giving to his customers thalers in place of his certificates of credit. When a customer had, let us say, five points' worth of goods due him, Peter Meyer would give him five thalers instead of a five point certificate of credit. He promised the customer that each silver thaler coin would be accepted by him as a payment for one point's worth of any of the goods he was offering for exchange.

By making that promise and applying that promise to *all* silver thalers, each coin became a certificate of credit for one point's worth of his goods. Each coin was the evidence of that promise; it was the evidence that the bearer had a claim for one point's worth of Peter Meyer's goods. It was accepted equally with the certificates of credit. Peter Meyer's verbal promise, which he applied to the silver thaler, was equal to his written promise on the certificate of credit. The silver thaler coin was the physical evidence of that promise.

After that promise was made and applied to every thaler coin, every thaler coin had two exchange values. It had the exchange value of a one-point certificate of credit issued by Peter Meyer and it had the exchange value of the silver content of the coin. Both of those exchange values were equal at that time. But both values did not remain equal.

PETER MEYER MADE A MISTAKE

Peter Meyer used poor judgment when he applied his promise to *all* thalers. He did not foresee that every thaler made by Count Schlick would become, in effect, his certificate of credit. Every thaler became the evidence of a claim for his goods. But the thalers were made by Count Schlick and Count Schlick had no right to issue certificates of credit against Peter Meyer's goods. Count Schlick did not intend that all the thalers he issued be used as certificates of credit against Peter Meyer's goods. Only the possessor of goods can, with justice, issue certificates of credit for the goods he possess.

Similarily, Peter Meyer had not intended to give Count Schlick the right to issue certificates of credit against his goods. But that is what happened when Peter Meyer promised to exchange his goods for all thalers at the rate of one point's worth of his goods for each thaler.

THE WORD "THALER" REPLACES THE WORD "POINT"

As more and more thalers came into circulation, Peter Meyer and his customers began speaking of thalers' worth of goods instead of points' worth of goods. And as each thaler was exchanged for one point's worth of goods and one point's worth of goods was exchanged for each thaler, it seemed to make good sense to use the word "thaler" as the name of the unit to express the exchange value of goods and services. A thaler was something that could be seen and put in a pocket.

Before the thaler came along, the point served very well as the name of the unit to express the exchange value of goods and services. Its meaning was understood. When the word "thaler" became the name of the unit that expressed exchange value, it tended to blur the meaning of the word "point." As time passed, the original meaning of the word "point" was forgotten.

It is important to note that for some years the word "thaler" was only the name of the coin. It was not the name of the unit used to express exchange value. Only when the word "thaler" replaced the word "point" as the name of the unit used to express the exchange value of goods and services, did the word "thaler" gain two meanings: 1. The silver coin. 2. The unit used to express exchange value.

After a large number of thaler coins were in circulation, Peter Meyer stopped issuing certificates of credit. For the customers the coins seemed to serve as a medium of exchange just as well as the certificates of credit. Besides being evidence of a claim for Peter Meyer's goods, they had the exchange value of their silver content; they had an impressive image of the patron saint of the village; and many people liked to possess them.

While most of the people used the thalers as a medium of exchange and as claims for Peter Meyer's goods, some people hoarded them for their silver content. Previously, the certificates of credit were not hoarded because they had only one value, which was as evidence of a claim for Peter Meyer's goods. And they had to be redeemed within one year from the date of issue.

For Peter Meyer the use of thalers required less bookkeeping than was necessary when he issued certificates of credit. So he decided to change his price tags from points to thalers.

When he marked the price tags in thalers (the exchange value) the price was expressed in monetary (coin) units as well as in the units used to express exchange value. That is, an item could be exchanged for a certain number of thaler coins or for the same number of points' (now thalers') worth of other goods.

When the exchange value was expressed only in points, it meant that an item could be exchanged for a certain number of points' worth of Peter Meyer's goods, including thaler coins.

Peter Meyer also changed his account books from points to thalers. By so doing, the word "thaler" then became the name of the unit of accounting. To Peter Meyer the change from certificates of credit to thaler coins and from points to thalers as units used to express exchange value seemed so logical and so simple that he did not realize the consequences. So let us list the consequences of those changes:

1. People lost the knowledge of the meaning of the word "point" as it was used to express the exchange value of goods and services.
2. The word "thaler" had two meanings: in one sense it meant the coin; in the other sense it meant the unit usedd to express exchange value. But the people understood only the one meaning, i.e., to them the word "thaler" meant only the thaler coin.
3. The exchange value of every item seemed to be expressed only in relation to the exchange value of the thaler coin. Previously, the point was used to express the exchange value of each item in relation to the exchange value of every other item, including thaler coins.
4. The thaler coins, which served as currency, were the evidence of claims for Peter Meyer's goods. But they were issued by Count Schlick who was not the possessor of the goods for which the thalers were the evidence of a claim.
5. Peter Meyer had forgotten how he issued and

used his certificates of credit. Others, too, forgot how they were issued and used as currency.

6. Count Schlick was the only person who issued the currency. He issued the claims against Peter Meyer's goods and Peter Meyer redeemed the claims. Peter Meyer no longer had full control over his goods.
7. Because the only currency then in circulation was the thaler coins, the exchange value (the price) of all goods and services had to be raised or lowered in proportion to the increase or decrease of the number of thaler coins placed in circulation by Count Schlick. Thus, Count Schlick, the only issuer of currency, was able to control all prices and the general business activity.
8. Because a record could be kept of the persons to whom and from whom certificates of credit were given or taken, the stealing of them was made difficult. With the use of coins, no such record could be kept. The result was that the stealing of coins was made easier than the stealing of the certificates of credit. For the same reason, the use of the coins for illegal purposes was made easier than when the certificates of credit were used.
9. If the exchange value of the silver in the thaler coin ever became greater than the exchange value of a thaler's worth of Peter Meyer's goods, the thaler would no longer be used as a medium of exchange. People would exchange it for the higher value.
10. If the exchange value of the silver in the thaler coin became less than one thaler's worth of Peter Meyer's goods, Count Schlick would obtain an unearned gain at the expense of all the other producers and distributors of goods and services, unless Peter Meyer and all others increased their prices.

None of these consequences was foreseen at the time by Peter Meyer or by the other people in the community. Count Schlick was mining silver and making silver objects, including coins. Other people were producing food, clothing, wool, shoes, and all the things the people needed. They were sharing (buying and selling) their goods with each other conveniently with the use of an adequate supply of coins. They had prosperity, not because the currency was silver thalers, but rather because they had a sufficient amount of currency.

But something else had taken place in the world. A man named Christopher Columbus discovered America in 1492 for Spain. When the Spaniards explored the new land, they discovered large deposits of silver in South America and in Mexico. They mined the silver and sold it all over the world. The result was a drop in the world price of silver.

When the people who had hoarded silver thalers tried to sell their thalers to silver buyers, they learned that their thalers would bring only 75% of the amount they formerly did. But at Peter Meyer's store they were accepted in exchange for other goods at the same rate as before because Peter Meyer had previously promised to accept them as if they were his certificates of credit at the exchange value of one point per thaler. The result was that many thalers (too many) were brought to Peter Meyer to be exchanged for his goods.

At the same time, the demand for Count Schlick's silver, his silver products, and his silver thalers was reduced. His business was declining. Peter Meyer could no longer accept his coins at the previous rate of exchange. So, in order for Count Schlick to have a market for his coins, he negotiated a deal with Peter Meyer whereby Peter Meyer would accept five silver thaler coins in exchange for the same items he formerly obtained for four thalers.

To carry out that deal, Peter Meyer raised the price of all his goods by 25%. The effect was that even though the thalers were expected to take the place of certificates of credit, they lost 25% of their exchange value when they were used as certificates. Had Peter

Meyer not raised his prices, however, he soon would have been sold out of all his goods at a loss of 25%.

If Peter Meyer had continued the use of certificates of credit with the point system, instead of the thaler system, the price of the silver thalers would have been reduced and all other prices would have remained unchanged. People would have understood clearly what had happened.

As it turned out, those people who had previously hoarded thalers and those who had previously loaned out thalers suffered a loss of buying power. Those people who had previously borrowed thalers obtained an unearned gain. And few, if any, understood the reasons why.

What went wrong? First, Count Schlick, with the cooperation of Peter Meyer, attempted to keep the thaler's exchange value as a silver item up to its exchange value as a certificate of credit, even after the exchange value of its silver content declined. That was accomplished by the increasing of all other prices.

Second, when too many thalers were brought to Peter Meyer to be redeemed (exchanged) for other goods, Peter Meyer did not have enough goods on hand to redeem those thalers unless he increased his prices.

If the point system had been kept as the means to express the exchange value of all goods, including the thaler coins, and if the certificates of credit had been kept as the items to serve as currency, no general price changes would have been necessary.

But when the exchange value of the thaler coins was fixed at a rate other than the market exchange value of their silver content, and the coins were used as a medium of exchange, the expressed exchange value (the price) of all other goods had to be adjusted according to the number of coins in circulation.

Instead of increasing prices by 25%, Peter Meyer could have said that since the price of silver declined by 25%, he would count each thaler coin as if it were 3/4 of a thaler. The people who held thalers would have had a

25% loss but the prices of all other items would not have had to be increased. But because he had given his promise (placed a fixed exchange value on the coins) that he would give one thaler's (point's) worth of his goods for each thaler coin, he could keep that promise only by raising all other prices.

Alternatively, instead of raising his prices by 25%, Peter Meyer could have insisted that the quantity of silver in each thaler coin brought to him be increased by 25%. Then no price increase would have been necessary. But, again, he would not have kept his promise.

A LESSON WAS LEARNED

Count Schlick learned a lesson from this experience. He learned that when more thalers were in circulation than the amount which would have been issued as bona fide certificates of credit, the general price level was increased.

He then decided that he would limit or control the number of coins he produced and offered for exchange. He would establish coin control or what some now call monetary control. In this way he was able to maintain reasonable stability in the general price level. That is he did until his mine began running low on silver.

As his mine was being depleted, his production of silver was reduced. He produced a smaller number of thalers and fewer thalers were placed in circulation. The price of silver increased. The general price level of all goods and services declined.

Peter Meyer's business also decreased. People did not have the normal number of thalers for the normal exchanging of goods and services. Does this not show how unwise it is for people to use a money system that can cause a slowdown in business and require the lowering of prices and wages in order to maintain normal business?

The ratio of circulating thalers to the goods and services being offered for exchange was out of balance.

The result was that the exchange value of each thaler was, in this new circumstance, increased. Similarly when the quantity of thalers in circulation was reduced, the persons who hoarded thalers and those who previously had loaned out thalers obtained an unearned gain. Those who previously had borrowed thalers suffered a loss because they had to produce more goods or services than before in order to earn the necessary thalers with which to pay their debts.

When Peter Meyer used the point as the unit to express the exchange value of goods, including coins, and issued certificates of credit which served as currency, there was no reason to have too many or too few certificates in circulation. The producers and the distributors of goods and services never suffered a loss because of too many (inflation) or too few (deflation) certificates of credit in circulation.

Certificates of credit were issued as the need for them arose and they were cancelled when they were redeemed for the goods for which they were issued as evidence of a claim. There was no need for monetary control or money management.

This is the end of the story of Peter Meyer and Count Schlick.

WHAT DID WE LEARN FROM THE STORY?

The experience of Peter Meyer, Count Schlick and the people of St. Joachimsthal illustrates that when goods are exchanged by direct barter, the exchange value of one item is expressed in relation to the exchange value of one or more other items. For example, one cow has the exchange value of 5 pigs, or 5 pigs have the exchange value of one cow. No common denominator unit is used to express the exchange value of all items. No common denominator unit is used to keep an account of the exchange value of all items. There is no unit of account.

The story also makes explicit the fact that in direct bartering each party to the transaction determines the exchange value of the items to be exchanged at the time the exchange is made. No third party, such as government or a bank, is involved in setting the exchange value (the price) on any of the items to be exchanged. No debts are incurred. No interest has to be paid for the use of currency. No balance of payment surplus or deficits can occur.

Other object lessons of the story of Joachimsthal are:

- When a practical common denominator unit was adopted to express the exchange value of all goods, services, and coins, it was an abstract unit called a point and that same unit, the point, served as the unit of account.
- Certificates of credit, using points as the units to express exchange value, could be issued by Peter Meyer as evidence of bona fide claims for his goods, and people used those certificates as their currency.
- The thaler coin had its origin in 1519 in Bohemia. It was called by similar names in various countries. In Spain it was called a dollar. (Later we shall learn that the people in the Spanish American colonies exchanged those dollar coins for goods from the English American colonies in such quantities that the word "dollar" was in common usage by the English Americans at the time of the Declaration of Independence.)
- When the thaler coin was given the status of a certificate of credit at the fixed price of one point, it then had two exchange values: the exchange value of its silver content and the exchange value of a certificate of credit for one point's worth of Peter Meyer's goods. When the two values were no longer equal, some people suffered an injustice.
- When currency is issued by one person and is redeemable with goods owned by a different person, the person who does the redeeming has lost much of his control over the exchanging of his goods. He is compelled to adjust his prices to bring them in balance with the quantity of currency that is placed

in circulation by the issuer of the currency. Furthermore, he may have to adjust the wages of the producers of his goods.

CHAPTER VII

THE POUND

About the year 775 A.D., the people of England adopted the word "pound" as the name of the unit which expressed the exchange value of coins and other goods and services. They used 925 parts of silver and 75 parts of copper to make a one-pound (by weight) block of alloy. From this one-pound block were coined 240 silver coins called "sterlings" or silver pennies. That alloy has since been called "sterling silver."

The exchange value of goods or services was expressed in "pounds of sterling." Later the term was shortened to "pounds sterling" and is frequently referred to as "pounds."

One-pound sterling silver coins were not made. The word "pound," therefore, was not the name of a coin. The sterling was the coin (monetary) unit. The word "pound" was the name of the unit used to express the exchange value of the coins and other goods and services. It also was the name of the unit used in accounting. The exchange value of goods, services, income, expenditures, and so on, is recorded in accounting by means of the unit that is used to express the exchange value of the items recorded.

The sterlings were coins, each with an exchange value of 1/240 pounds or pounds sterling. These coins served as a medium of exchange.

In later years, England made many different coins. In 1351, England made a gold coin called a "noble." That was a coin (monetary) unit. England also made gold coins called half nobles and quarter nobles. The noble, at that time, had 120 grains of gold with an expressed exchanged value of 1/3 pound. In 1489, England made a coin with 240 grains of gold, called a "sovereign," with an expressed exchange value of one pound sterling. The shilling was issued about the year 1504. There were times when England made coins called "crowns," "groats," "florins," and "double florins." These were gold or silver coins upon which the government placed a fixed value. When the market value of the metal in these coins became higher than the government-fixed value, the coins were exchanged for the higher market value and no longer circulated as media of exchange.

All of these coins were properly called units of coins or monetary units, but the names of these coins were not officially used as the names of units to express exchange value. The exchange value of these coins was expressed in pounds, or pounds sterling, or fractions thereof, a fact that provides further proof that the pound or pound sterling was not a monetary unit but the name of the abstract unit used to express the exchange value of the coins as well as the exchange value of other goods and services. To call the pound the British monetary unit, as some writers do, does not make it so. It is correct to call the pound the British unit of account because the unit is used in accounting.

AN EARLY ENGLISH CURRENCY

About the year 1100 A.D., the English government issued items which were used as currency but which did not consist of coins or paper bills. They were made of wooden sticks called "tally sticks."

The sticks were issued directly by the government as payment for goods and services purchased by the government. They were the equivalent of what we call tax credit certificates. They were, in effect, bona fide documents "written" by means of cutting notches in the wooden sticks. They gave evidence of the amount of pounds worth of due taxes for which they would be received as payment.

From the time they were issued as a payment for goods or services rendered to the government until they were redeemed as payment for taxes, they served the people as currency.

The following quotation is taken from the 1913 edition of *The Century Dictionary and Cyclopedia*:

TALLY

"A piece of wood on which notches or scores are cut to mark numbers, as in keeping an account or giving a receipt; loosely, anything on which a score or account is kept.

"Before the use of writing, or before writing became general, this or something like it was the usual method of keeping accounts. In purchasing and selling it was customary to make duplicate tallies of the transaction, or to split one tally through the middle.

"In the English Exchequer (Treasury) tallies were used until 1812, which answered the purpose of receipts as well as simple records of matters of account.

"An Exchequer tally was an account of a sum of money lent to the government, or a sum for which the government would be responsible.

"The tally itself consisted of a square rod of hazel or other wood, having on one side notches indicating the sum for which the tally was an acknowledgment. On two other sides, opposite to each other, the amount of the sum, the name of the payer, and the date of the transaction were written by an officer called the writer of the tallies. This being done, the rod was then cleft longitudinally in such a manner that each piece retained one of the written sides, and one-half of each notch cut in the tally.

"One of these parts, the *counterfoil* or *counterstock*, was kept in the Exchequer, and only the other, the stock, issued. When the part issued was returned to the Exchequer (usually as a payment of taxes) the two parts were compared, as a check against fraudulent imitation. This was called tally or tallies.

"The size of the notches made on the tallies varied with the amounts. The notch for 100 pounds was the breadth of a thumb; the 1 pound notch, the breadth of a barleycorn. A penny was indicated by a slight slit."

More details on the issuing and use of tally sticks are given by Gertrude M. Coogan in *Money Creators* beginning on page 313.[1]

"ENGLISH TALLIES:

"This form of national money was adopted in England as the means of financing the government, by Henry the First, fourth son of William the Conqueror. Henry I ascended the throne in the year 1100 A.D.

"The 'tallies' were made of wood, being four-sided rods of hazel or linden wood about an inch thick. The amount due from the state to the payee was designated by notches cut into one of the flat sides, and also written in ink on the two adjacent sides. The piece was then split lengthwise through the notches, so that each piece carried ink markings of value.

"One piece was *paid* out to the payee; the matching piece being retained in the treasury as a method of preventing counterfeiting.

"STATE MONEY

"All who served the king or state were paid in these tallies, enough being issued so that they could be paid out until tax collection time again brought in this money for state use. Supplies for the royal household were also purchased by the issuing of these tallies, which circulated among merchants and people, being used in the exchange of commodities and services.

---

[1]Excerpt from Gertrude M. Coogan, *Money Creators*, Omni Publications, by permission of Omni Publications, P.O. Box 216, Hawthorne, California 90250.

"At tax collection time the sheriff of each county called all who had exchequer tallies to present them and obtain allowances for them. They were matched with the counter-tallies. When the edges matched, they were said to 'tally,' hence the name.

"Their sole value was derived from their acceptability by the people in payment for any kind of goods and services, which in turn was derived solely from the acceptability as (payment for) taxes (levied) by the government which had paid them into circulation in the first place.

"USED FOR CENTURIES

"These tallies were used as money by the people of England for 594 years, exclusively; for the next 89 years partially, and for another 43 years unofficially, a total of 726 years. This is a tribute to their usefulness and acceptability, and political soundness, which may well be marked by the advocates of the gold standard, an infant in comparison. It will be noted that the incidence of violent depressions is traced back, in all modern treatises, only a little over one hundred years; which period corresponds accurately with the use of the gold standard.

"The Bank 'of England' was chartered in 1694. There were then about $70,000,000 in wooden tallies in circulation. The new bank was given the original privilege of issuing paper money, loaning it into circulation, and collecting interest on its creations. The plain fact was that there were not enough tallies in circulation! At any rate, the new private money did not seem dangerous, because no one could get it without paying interest. It turned out, however, to be a case of the camel being allowed first to put his toe inside the tent which was followed by further extension of privilege until the camel alone was *in* the tent, the master having been crowded out.

"A weak king could not defend himself; parliamentary hirelings of the money creators did the rest.

"Naturally, the use of the more convenient paper

bank money after a time displaced the cumbersome wooden tallies, some of which were two or four feet in length.

"In 1783 the use of tallies was abolished by an Act of Parliament. America was free but England sank deeper into false money principles and hence slavery!

"In spite of this, however, tallies were continued until 1826. In 1830 the heaps of broken tallies were ordered burned in the furnaces of the Houses of Parliament. A defective or overheated flue started a fire which completely destroyed the buildings.

"One of the tallies is still preserved in the British Museum. Edmund Burke mentions tallies in his Speech of Conciliation.

"And note well, that the value of the tallies was acknowledged by the incorporators of the Bank 'of England,' for, in 1697, when the capital was increased, $800,000 of the new capital was paid for with the wooden tallies. They were accepted at par.

"The English tallies were another form of sound money maneuvered out of existence by the privately owned Bank of England. The Bank of England usurped the prerogative of money issuance, and its owners caused the tallies to be taken out of use."

SUMMARY

When the word "pound" was adopted in England in the year 775 as the name of the unit used to express the exchange value of goods and services, it really expressed the market exchange value (the price) of one pound of sterling silver. The exchange values of all goods and services were expressed in the ratio of their exchange values to what was then the exchange value of one pound of sterling silver. The result of establishing that ratio was that the exchange value of each item had a definite ratio to the exchange value of every other item. Items equal to the same thing are equal to each other. Thus, items having a definite ratio of exchange value to the exchange value of one pound of sterling silver will have a definite ratio of exchange value to the exchange value of each other.

That exchange value may be accurately expressed by using that common denominator unit called the pound. The unit called the pound served the same purpose in England that the unit called the point served when Peter Meyer first used it to express the exchange value of the goods in his store.

After some time passed and the ratio of the exchange value of each item was well established in relation to the exchange value of other items, it was no longer necessary for the exchange value of a pound, by weight, of sterling silver to remain constant.

The exchange value of sterling silver did not remain constant, but the term "pound" or "pound sterling" continued to serve as the name of the unit used to express the exchange value of all goods, coins, and services, including the exchange value of a pound, by weight, of sterling silver.

In 1973 a pound, by weight, of sterling silver had an exchange value of about seven pounds or pounds sterling. Note the two different meanings of the term "pound sterling."

When it was announced that the pound had lost value, it meant that the exchange value of the currency, which was expressed in pounds, lost value. The term "pound" (or pound sterling) was the name of the abstract unit used to express the exchange value of the currency, but it had no exchange value in itself. Therefore, it had no exchange value to lose.

In the preceding descriptions of tally sticks and their function, it was shown that currency may be issued by a government without gold, without silver, and without borrowing.

Today, in place of tally sticks, a governmental body could issue tax credit certificates which would serve the same purpose that tally sticks served. They would be as convenient and acceptable as the present Federal Reserve notes.

CHAPTER VIII

THE DOLLAR COIN AND THE DOLLAR UNIT WE USE TO EXPRESS EXCHANGE VALUE

After Spain discovered large amounts of silver in its colonies in Mexico and South America, the Spanish government made many silver coins. The silver coin made by Spain and used in large quantities throughout the Spanish-American colonies in trade with the English-American colonies was called the Spanish milled dollar. It was a large silver coin which at one time weighed 423.45 grains and at another time 417.28 grains. In 1786 and for some years thereafter, it contained 375.64 grains of pure silver.

The first United States silver dollar coin authorized by Congress in 1792 weighed 416 grains and had 89.24% silver content. After 1837 the coin weighed 412.5 grains and had 90% silver content. Both coins had 371.25 grains of pure silver.

In addition to the Spanish milled dollar coin, Spain also made a smaller silver coin called a "real." It too circulated extensively in the English-American colonies. The real was also called a "bit." One quarter dollar was two reals or two bits. A Spanish milled dollar was the equivalent of eight reals.

Because the Spanish-American colonies had an unfavorable balance of trade with the English-American colonies, the Spanish milled dollar was the predominant coin in circulation in the English-American colonies. These coins had the exchange value of their silver content. They were items used as goods are in bartering. They were not the evidence of claims for anything. They were not tokens, certificates of credit, or tax credit certificates. Governmental bodies did accept them, however, as payment for taxes and for other charges due the government at the exchange value (the market value) of their silver content.

Some of the colonies even declared the Spanish milled dollars to be legal tender at the market value of their silver content. In 1857, Congress repealed the legal tender power of all foreign coins.

CONTINENTAL CURRENCY

When the Continental Congress issued the bills which were to serve as the Continental currency, the following words were inscribed on the face of the bills:

THIS BILL
entitles the Bearer to receive
SIX SPANISH MILLED DOLLARS,
or the Value thereof in GOLD or SILVER,

according to a Resolution of CONGRESS
published at Philadelphia Nov. 2, 1776.

THE WORD "DOLLAR"—THE OFFICIAL NAME OF THE UNIT USED IN THE UNITED STATES TO EXPRESS EXCHANGE VALUE

The Spanish milled dollar coin was so widely used in the English-American colonies that people were using the word "dollar," not only as the name of the coin, but also as the name of the unit with which to express the exchange value of goods, services, and other currencies. The word "dollar" was so well established in its usage as the name of the common denominator unit with which to express exchange values, that on July 6, 1785, the United States Congress meeting under the Articles of Confederation, declared the word "dollar" the official name of the unit of account that was to be used in the United States.

The Congress called it the United States monetary

(coin) unit. But it was not the name of a United States coin at that time because the United States dollar coin was not authorized to be minted until 1792. It was correct to call the word "dollar" the unit of account because the unit used in accounting is the unit used to express the exchange value of the items listed in accounts.

At that time, when the unit called a dollar was used to express exchange value, it meant the amount of the exchange value (the market value) of the silver in the Spanish milled dollar.

The word "dollar" was the name given to the abstract unit or concept or device that served the same purpose for the people in the English-American colonies as the "point" served for Peter Meyer when he first established it as the name of the common denominator unit with which he expressed his idea of the exchange value of his goods. It served the same function the English unit "pound" served when it was first established as the name of the unit expressing exchange value.

When the early Americans first used the word "dollar" as the name of the unit with which to express the exchange value of goods and services, it meant the exchange value of the silver content of the Spanish milled dollar in relation to the exchange value of other items. They could have used the word "point" or "unit" and said that each Spanish milled dollar coin was worth, or was equal to, one point's or one unit's worth of the item to which it was applied and thus expressed the exchange value of all goods and services with points or units in the same ratio as with the unit they called the dollar.

We know that the word "point" or "unit" by itself has no exchange value. When the word "dollar" is used as the name of the unit to express exchange value, it too has no exchange value. In fact, it has no meaning unless it is applied to something which has exchange value.

When one asks a teller in a bank for one hundred dollars, it is unlikely that either the customer or the teller understands that the bank does not possess any dollars. The bank may possess coins, notes, or certificates, but these should not be called dollars. The teller will, however, ask the customer, "How do you want the hundred dollars?"

A bank customer using correct terminology would reply, "I would like fifty dollars' worth of one-dollar Federal Reserve notes, ten dollars' worth of Eisenhower dollar coins, ten dollars' worth of half-dollar coins, ten dollars' worth of one-quarter dollar coins, ten dollars' worth of dimes, and ten dollars' worth of nickels." The amounts of each monetary unit may vary, but the names of the units would be accurate. Thus, the hypothetical customer receives not one hundred dollars but one hundred dollars' worth of notes and coins. The word "dollar" or "dollars" is used correctly as an adjective, not a noun. It must be applied to something before it has any meaning. In the case illustrated above it is applied to notes and coins. The Eisenhower dollar coins are not dollars; they are coins.

Let us give another illustration: If a person owes you $4 and offers to give you forty 10¢ postage stamps as payment, you might accept them. People do accept postage stamps for certain payments. There is no reason why postage stamps could not be used as currency. In 1863, during a shortage of fractional (small denomination) coins, postage stamps were widely used as currency in the United States.

If postage stamps were commonly used as currency, and one acquired $100 worth of stamps, he might decide to deposit them in his checking account at a bank. Then, if he wrote a check for $10, he would be giving the bank an order to pay to the payee of the check $10 worth of postage stamps (which, as currency, could be used by the payee to purchase other goods and services).

It is in the same manner that, when we now write a check for $10, we give an order to the bank to pay to the payee $10 worth of currency (coins or notes). The bank does not pay out dollars. It pays out dollars' worth of currency. Dollars are not currency.

Postage stamps are received by the postoffice as payment for postal service. Coins and notes are received by the government as payment for taxes and other charges due the government.

Postage stamps, coins, United States notes, and Federal Reserve notes may be used as currency and their exchange value is expressed as dollars' worth of stamps, or dollars' worth of coins, or dollars' worth of United States notes, or dollars' worth of Federal Reserve notes.

We should not be surprised when we are told that the unit (the dollar) used to express exchange value has no exchange value in itself. When we study the units used in other fields, we find they too have no value or meaning until they are applied to things.

Numbers have no meaning until they are applied to things. The numbers 2, 10, or 100 by themselves mean nothing. One does not say, "I have two, ten, or one hundred." Such a statement is meaningless. But if one says, "I have two cars, ten children, and 100 chickens," he is giving meaningful information.

Likewise, the unit used to express (not measure) weight—the pound—has no weight. Scales are used to measure the weight of an object; then the weight is expressed in pounds or other units used to express weight.

The unit to express length, the yard, has no meaning until it is applied to something. One cannot buy yards. One may buy yards of something. A yardstick is used to measure the length of an item and then the length is expressed in yards. There is a difference between the yardstick and the yard, the unit used to express the length of the yardstick. Likewise, the dollar coin and the unit, dollar, used to express exchange value, are two different things.

Let us give another illustration by comparing the dollar unit to express exchange value with a unit we use to express volume, the gallon.

If a person says that he has a gallon jug, the word "gallon" is used as an adjective. It describes the noun, jug. If a person says that he has a gallon of water, the word "gallon" is used as a noun. It is the name of a unit we use to express a certain volume. A person does not say, "I have a gallon," because a gallon as a unit to express volume does not exist as a physical thing. The unit called gallon exists only as a concept.

The same is true for the unit we call a dollar. When the word "dollar" is used as the name of the concept or device we use as a common denominator unit to express the exchange value of goods, services, and currencies, it is used as a noun. When the word "dollar" is used to describe a Federal Reserve note or a coin, it is used as an adjective.

When we use the word "dollar" as a noun, it is the name of a concept. It has no meaning unless it is applied to something, just as the word "gallon" has no meaning unless it is applied to something. A person cannot buy a gallon. He cannot carry a gallon. He cannot store a gallon. But a person may buy, carry, or store a gallon of something.

Similarly, a person does not receive dollars from a bank. He does not carry dollars in his pockets. He does not store dollars in his safe. But a person may receive, carry, or store dollars' worth of currency (coins or notes) because items of currency are physical things; they are not concepts.

When we hear the statement, "the dollar lost value," we should understand that it does not tell us anything. We know that the dollar unit did not and could not lose value because the unit, being a concept, has no exchange value to lose. What is meant by the statement "the dollar lost value," is that the currency, the exchange value of which is expressed in dollar units, lost exchange value.

The question might be asked, for what purpose is the dollar unit used? The dollar unit was and is used to express the ratio of the exchange value of one item to the exchange value of another item.

For example, a dollar bill has a specific exchange value, one dollar's worth, when it is used as a payment for taxes. But when it is used to buy goods and services, it will have the amount of exchange value to which the buyer and seller agree at the time of the transaction.

As an illustration, let us say a person offers to sell his potatoes for one dollar bill per bushel. The one dollar bill will have the exchange value of one bushel of potatoes. If, at a later date, he offers to sell the potatoes for two one-dollar bills per bushel, each dollar bill will then have the exchange value of only one-half bushel of potatoes. The dollar unit was used to express the two different ratios of the exchange values of the dollar bills and the potatoes.

We should note that the exchange value of both the dollar bills and the bushel of potatoes changed between the first transaction and the second transaction. The dollar unit was used to express the different ratios of exchange value of the dollar bills and the bushel of potatoes in both transactions.

When people in the early days of our country decided to use the exchange value of the silver dollar coin as the exchange value to be expressed with the dollar unit, the unit expressed the exchange value of the coin. The silver dollar coin was intended to be the embodiment of the concept unit called the dollar. It remained so only as long as the price of silver did not increase or decrease. When the price of silver changed, the unit called the dollar might just as well have been called a unit or a point because it served only as an abstract unit to express the exchange value of one item in its relation to the exchange value of other items.

Once the ratio of the exchange value of each item is established in relation to the exchange value of other items, the exchange value of all items, including currency, can be expressed with an abstract unit called a unit, a point, or any other name, as well as the unit called the dollar.

CHAPTER IX

UNITED STATES COINAGE

When the United States government first made gold and silver coins, it did not make the coins for its own use. It did not make the coins so that it could use them as payments for its expenses. It made the coins for the people who brought gold and silver to the mint for the purpose of having the metal made into coins for their own use. They were the ones who would use the coins as payments to the government and to others.

The amount of coins minted by the government was limited to production from the gold and silver brought to the mint. That production was not sufficient to provide an adequate supply of the medium of exchange. That is why foreign coins circulated in large quantities until 1854.

The United States mint began making coins in 1794. Anyone, including banks, could and did bring gold and silver to the mint for the purpose of having it made into coins. The coins did not belong to the government. The coins were given to those who brought in the metal. They were the owners of the coins and could do with them whatever they wished.

But what happened! When the coins were minted, Congress immediately declared the coins to have a fixed legal tender exchange value. The result was that between 1794 and 1834 very few United States coins were in circulation. Not until 1853, when the fractional silver coins (coins with a face value less than one dollar) were made token coins by reducing their silver content by 7%, did an abundance of United States fractional silver coins circulate. The Spanish silver coins circulated until 1857.

Why, during those years, did the foreign coins circulate, although not in sufficient quantity, and the United States coins did not? Was it not the intention of the writers of the Constitution that the value of the United States minted coins be regulated in the same manner as the foreign coins? We know that the Congress did not regulate or adjust the exchange value, the legal tender value, of the United States coins in the same manner as it did the foreign coins. The Congress fixed the exchange value, the legal tender value, of the United States coins at the time it authorized the minting of the coins, instead of at the time they were used as a payment.

It probably did not occur to the members of Congress that the exchange value (the price) of gold and silver would change. Thus, the members of Congress, perhaps without being aware of it, did not follow the intentions of the writers of the Constitution. That is, they did not regulate the value of the United States coins as they did the foreign coins.

The United States Congress did not (of course, it could not) place an exchange value on the foreign coins at the time they were minted. The United States government placed on the foreign coins the market value of their metal content only at the time the foreign coins were used as payments.

It will serve us well to remember that when we either barter directly or buy and sell, the effective time for us to place an exchange value on the items to be exchanged is at the time the exchange is made.

Coins are items we exchange. They are not different from other items, unless a government unwisely declares them to have a legal tender value, that is different from the market value of their metal content.

Instead of waiting to declare the market value of their metal content as the legal tender value of the first United States gold and silver coins at the time the coins were presented as payments, Congress set the legal tender value of the coins at the market value of their metal content at the time it authorized the minting of the coins in 1792.

By 1794, when the coins were first minted, and for many years thereafter, the market value of gold and silver increased so that the coins were worth more as bullion than the previously set legal tender value. So the people exchanged the newly minted United States coins for the higher market value. That is why the coins did not circulate as currency. On the other hand, the legal tender value of the foreign coins was adjusted (regulated) so that it was equal to the market value of the metal content of the coins at the time the coins were used as a payment. That is why they did circulate as currency. There was no higher value for which they could be exchanged.

If the government had regulated the exchange value of the gold and silver coins to conform to the market value of their metal content at the time the coins were used as payments, just as it did with foreign coins, the coins would have circulated to this day because there never would have been a higher value for which they could be exchanged.

Whenever a person has justly acquired gold or silver coins, the coins belong to him. He is free to exchange them for other items at any exchange value that is acceptable to the person with whom he is making exchanges. It is not a function of the government to fix an exchange value on gold or silver coins until they are used as payments to the government or by the government.

In the Coinage Act of 1792, the United States Congress provided for the establishing of a mint and the authorizing of the minting of full bodied legal tender gold and silver coins and token copper coins. The exchange value of the coins was to be expressed in the unit authorized on July 6, 1785, namely, the dollar.

The silver dollar coin was declared to have a legal tender exchange value of one exchange value unit, that is, one dollar. So when the first silver dollar coin was issued in 1794, it had the words "HUNDRED CENTS, ONE DOLLAR OR UNIT" stamped on the edge of the coin. Thus, this large silver coin was designated as a dollar unit or dollar coin.

We must distinguish between the two meanings of the word "dollar." When it describes the coin, it is used as an adjective; when it is used as the name of our unit to express exchange value, it is used as a noun. It is correct to say that our largest coin is a dollar coin. In that sentence the word "dollar" is used as an adjective. It is also correct to say that the word "dollar" is the name of the unit we use to express exchange value. The word "dollar" is used in that sentence as a noun.

The gold coin unit was given a different name. It was called the "eagle." Gold coins called the eagle, double eagle, half eagle, and quarter eagle were made. The eagle was the name of the monetary (coin) unit for gold coins.

The government gave the eagle coin the legal tender exchange value of ten exchange value units, or ten dollars; a double-eagle coin twenty dollars; a half-eagle coin, five dollars; and a quarter-eagle coin, two and one-half dollars.

The eagle was not the name of an official unit of account, although the Congress could have made it so. The people themselves could have made it a unit with which to express exchange value by using it as such. Prices could be expressed in eagles and in fractions of eagles just as well as in dollars and in fractions of dollars.

When the Congress in 1792 authorized the mint to make the gold and silver coins full bodied coins, the market value of the metal in the coins was equal to their legal tender value. History shows that such coins will be used as a medium of exchange only so long as the market value of their metal content does not exceed their legal tender value.

Gold and silver full bodied coins would be very useful as a medium of exchange and they would stay in circulation if the weight of the metal was stamped on the coin and the government would not give the coins any fixed legal tender exchange value. If the government is to give full bodied coins a legal tender value, it should declare the legal tender value of the coins to be the market value of the metal in the coins at the time the coins are used as a payment. In that way it would be following the Constitution by regulating the exchange value of the coins at the proper times, instead of fixing the exchange value of the coins at the time the coins are minted.

The first silver dollar coins minted in 1794 contained 371.25 grains of pure silver. That was the standard silver dollar coin to which all silver dollar coins had to conform. The government at that time set the exchange value of the coin for legal tender purposes at one dollar. That was the market exchange value of its silver content at that time. But, by 1804, the price of silver increased so much that some people and some foreign governments were offering a price higher than one dollar for the coin. The result was that the mint made no silver dollar coins from 1804 to 1835 because those coins that were made before 1804 were not being used as a medium of exchange. They were being exchanged for a higher exchange value as fast as they were being minted. Many were exchanged for the Spanish milled dollar coin which contained 4.39 more grains of pure silver than the United States silver dollar coin.

The first gold coin Congress authorized to be minted was the eagle. It was to be made with 247.5 grains of pure gold. It was the standard gold coin to which all gold coins had to conform. The first gold coin actually minted by the United States mint, however, was the half Eagle in 1795. It contained 123.75 grains of pure gold. It was given a legal tender value of $5 or $1 for each 24.75 grains of pure gold. But the value of "5 D" was not stamped on the coin until 1807. The value "TEN D" was not stamped on the eagle until 1838.

The legal tender exchange value for the gold coins at the rate of $1 for each 24.75 grains of pure gold might have been the market value of the gold at the time the Congress authorized the minting of the coins in 1792, but a few years later the market value of the gold was higher than the legal tender value, so only a few gold coins circulated as currency.

In fact only a small number of half eagles were minted between 1795 and 1834. No eagle coins were minted between 1805 and 1836. In the Gold Bill of 1834 Congress increased the legal tender value of the gold coins to about the market value of their gold content by reducing the number of grains of gold for each dollar of legal tender exchange value from 24.75 grains to 23.2 grains.

In 1837, Congress slightly reduced the legal tender exchange value of the gold coins by increasing the gold content for each $1 legal tender value from 23.20 to 23.22 grains. Gold coins were then minted in quantity and circulated as currency.

TOKEN COINS

Token coins are those coins that have a face value or a legal tender value which is greater than the market value of their metal content. They may or may not contain gold or silver. For many years before 1964 the United States silver coins had a high silver content but they still were token coins because the market value of their silver content was less than their face or legal tender value. Since 1972 all newly minted coins in circulation are token coins made with copper and/or nickel.

Before 1933 token coins were legal tender only for small payments, but they were exchangeable for full bodied gold coins. In 1933 all coins were declared to be legal tender for large or small payments, but they were no longer exchangeable for gold coins.

Government officials can with honesty and with justice place token coins into circulation in two ways:

1. They can accept and safekeep for any person full bodied gold or silver coins and give in exchange token coins as evidence of "on demand claims" for the gold or silver coins they are holding for safekeeping. Those token coins would be, in effect, warehouse receipts.

2. Government officials can pay out token coins as

payments for goods and services, levy a tax for the amount paid out, and at taxpaying time redeem them as the payment for the then due taxes. These coins would be, in effect, tokens serving as tax credit certificates.

In both cases the token coins would be bona fide because they would be redeemable either in full bodied coins or as payment for taxes. As long as government officials redeemed the token coins, they would not cause an inflation of the currency and they would serve as an acceptable medium of exchange.

CONGRESS SEEMED TO DECLARE THE DOLLAR TO BE A SPECIFIC NUMBER OF GRAINS OF GOLD

When a person deposits an item with someone for safekeeping, he expects to get back that same item when he calls for it. When you check your coat in a check-room, you are given a token with a number on it. That token is the evidence of your claim for your coat.

Before 1933, when a person deposited gold at a United States Mint or Assay Office and received gold certificates as the evidence of his claim for the gold, he expected to get back, when he or the bearer of the gold certificates called for it, the same number of grains or ounces of gold that he deposited.

When the government issued gold certificates, however, and when the Federal Reserve Banks and others issued notes that were payable in gold, those certificates and notes gave evidence of the claims in dollars' worth of gold. They did not give evidence of claims for grains or ounces of gold as bona fide warehouse receipts would have done.

Therefore, in order for the depositors and other claimants to reclaim or receive as payment the correct amount of gold by weight, it was necessary for government officials to declare by law the number of grains of gold that should be given for each one-dollar claim or payment.

From that it followed that all promises to pay in gold

or in dollars' worth of gold meant that each dollar's worth of gold was a certain number of grains of gold. Although it may seem so, this is not equivalent to declaring the dollar, which is the unit we use to express exchange value, to have a certain number of grains of gold. What really happened was that government officials had by law declared a fixed price on gold.

Between 1792 and 1834 a dollar's worth of gold was declared to be 24.75 grains of gold, between 1834 and 1837 it was 23.20 grains, and between 1837 and 1934 it was 23.22 grains. After January 1934, it was declared to be 13.71 grains of pure gold for those who were allowed to buy or sell it.

The government had to establish a specific number of grains of gold as worth a dollar in gold certificates and other items used as currency which were payable in gold, or else the gold certificates and other items payable in gold would have had to be payable in grains or ounces of gold.

What the government did caused no injustice for those who had deposited gold with the United States government, but it may have caused injustice to borrowers of funds because they had to make future payments in gold at the price of gold at the time the payments were due.

Let us consider the two cases: In the first, when a person deposits gold with the government, or anyone else, it was fair for him to ask for and to expect to receive the same amount of gold that he deposited because the gold was his. He was justified in expecting it to be there. The cost of its production and transportation was completed.

In the second case, involving the borrowing of funds, the individual was expected to make payments over a period of years with a certain number of ounces of gold. The gold for those future payments may have to be mined and refined and transported at an unknown cost. The mine may become depleted and the cost for obtaining that number of ounces of gold from someone else for those future payments may become exceedingly high.

In such a case the loaner by receiving his payments in

ounces of gold instead of in dollars' worth of gold at the market price, may receive much more than his just payment by dint of the unjustly increased payments the borrower may be forced to make.

When the government sets a specific number of grains of gold for each future dollar payment, it may cause an injustice to the payer. If the government does not set a specific number of grains of gold for each future dollar payment, and the currency becomes inflated, it may cause an injustice to the payee.

Clearly, the moral here is: let both buyer and seller beware when they make agreements for future payments!

FUTURE PAYMENTS

The items we use as currency serve to make indirect bartering (buying and selling) convenient. Generally speaking, in bartering or buying and selling we are expected to complete the transaction at one time. The currency we use is intended for that purpose. It might be more accurate to say that we should expect our items of currency to serve within the present time framework. There is no currency now available which would serve with certainty five or ten years from now as just payment for a debt incurred today. Governments have declared some currencies to be legal tender. By law, then, long term debts can be legally paid with legal tender, but in some cases such payments may be unjust settlements.

Let us postulate that we are using one-ounce gold coins as our currency and that at 1976 prices a single one-ounce gold coin will buy 35 bushels of wheat, or four pairs of men's shoes, or 200 gallons of gasoline. Who can be sure how much of any one of these items that same one-ounce gold coin will buy five or ten years hence? If we cannot be sure that a one-ounce gold coin will buy the same amount of goods or services five or ten years hence, then what other type of currency would?

A bushel of wheat, a barrel of salt, a 1,000-pound steer, a gallon of gasoline, or an hour's labor may not have the same exchange value five, ten, or twenty years from now as it now has. Similarly, a document such as a warehouse receipt, giving evidence of a claim for any of those items also would not have the same exchange value five, ten or twenty years in the future. This shows us the problem we face when we attempt to make a contract for a just future payment.

It is generally said that future payments are to be made in dollars' worth of legal tender. History should have taught us that when government officials take it upon themselves to ignore the Constitution and declare anything they wish to be legal tender, people have no assurance what will be legal tender at some future date. We know the Congress of the United States has changed the laws regarding legal tender on many occasions.

We know that, ultimately, all payments are made with goods or services. Why, then, would it not be wise to make our agreements for future payments to be made in dollars' worth of goods or services?

For example, let us say, a farmer purchases some goods at a general store. The merchant allows the farmer to pay for the goods at a later date with farm produce. When the farmer brings in his produce as payment, the exchange value (the price) of the produce will be determined at its market value at the time the payment is made, not at the market price of the produce at the time the agreement was made.

Although no currency exists which is certain to serve as just payment in the future, a reasonably just arrangement can be made by agreeing to accept future payments in dollars' worth of goods or services, the exchange value of which will be their market value at the time the payment is made.

The only weakness in that idea is the fact that we allow inflationary currency and inflationary bank credit to serve legally as media of exchange.

If tax credit certificates and certificates of credit were issued in good faith, however, and were used as media of exchange, there would be no legal inflationary media of exchange.

CHAPTER X

MONEY AND THE CONSTITUTION

ARTICLE I, SECTION 8, CLAUSE 1

"The Congress shall have Power to lay and collect Taxes . . ." This clause of the United States Constitution gives Congress the power to lay and collect taxes in order to pay for the government's needed expenditures. With these powers Congress decides what items it will use to pay for the expenditures and what the people will use to pay those taxes. If honesty is practiced, the Congress must receive as payment for those taxes the same items it used to pay for its expenditures.

In this clause the Constitution gives Congress the power to issue tax credit certificates and to receive and redeem those certificates when they are presented as payment for taxes.

If governmental bodies do not issue tax credit certificates for the purpose of paying for their needed expenditures, they cannot operate unless they incur interest-bearing debts, or wait until taxpaying time to pay their bills, or require the taxpayers to pay their taxes in advance.

The issuance of tax credit certificates would enable a governmental body to pay for its expenses concurrently and also lighten the taxpayers' burden because no interest-bearing debts would be incurred and enough certificates (currency) would be in circulation to pay the taxes. An additional benefit would be the free use of these certificates as a medium of exchange.

ARTICLE I, SECTION 8, CLAUSE 2

"The Congress shall have Power . . . to borrow Money on the credit of the United States: . . ."

In order for the members of Congress to adhere to the Constitution when they plan to borrow money, they must understand what the writers of the Constitution meant by the word "money." They must know what items of currency the government can lawfully borrow.

In chapter I it was noted that at the time the Constitution was written the word "money" meant coins and only coins. The Constitution did not say that the Congress shall have power to borrow unredeemable bank notes or bank credit. Bank credit is make-believe money.

When the United States government borrows bank credit from Federal Reserve banks or from commercial banks, the government's account is credited for the amount borrowed. The government, on its part, gives the bank a United States interest-bearing bond, note, or bill for that credit.

The government spends such bank credit by issuing checks and creating greater buying power; should there be insufficient increase in the amount of goods and/or services being offered for sale, an inflation of the purchasing media occurs and abnormally high prices are the result. It does not appear likely that the writers of the Constitution intended to give Congress that kind of power.

If the government officials borrow real money which someone has earned and spend it, no inflation will occur and no increase in the general price level will result because there will be no increase in the money supply.

While the Constitution gives Congress the power to borrow real earned money (not bank credit) there is no need to do so because the government can pay for whatever goods or services it needs by issuing interest-free bona fide tax tax credit certificates.

ARTICLE I, SECTION 8, CLAUSE 5

"The Congress shall have Power . . . to coin Money, regulate the Value thereof, and of foreign Coin, and fix the Standard of Weights and Measures; . . ."

The above section of the Constitution is frequently quoted but seldom explained. We are not able to ask the writers of the Constitution what they meant by that clause, so let us, by studying the monetary customs and usages of the period, try to deduce the meaning they had in mind.

Note that the Constitution does not say, "to regulate the value of the dollar." Dollars are not coins. The Constitution does not specify the number of coins to be minted. It does not stipulate that the amount of coins to be minted should correspond to the amount of goods and services being offered for sale; nor does it indicate how the coins are to be placed in circulation. It does not grant Congress the power to set a *fixed* exchange value on the coins. Finally, and perhaps most important, it does not designate when and how the exchange value of the coins should be regulated.

To begin our study let us return to the verb "to coin," which means to make coins. In the usage of the period when the Constitution was written, the expression, "to coin money" meant to make coins. The word "money" meant coins, not notes or certificates. "To coin money" did not and does not mean any of the following:

1. To issue United States notes.
2. To issue Federal Reserve notes.
3. To issue tax credit certificates.
4. To provide the government and the people with all the media of exchange they need.
5. To declare anything to be legal tender.
6. To operate banks.
7. To establish a Monetary Commission (The Federal Reserve System) to increase and decrease the

"money supply" (secretly) for the government and the people.
8. To store gold and silver and then issue certificates which are a combination of warehouse receipts, certificates of credit, and certificates of legal tender.
9. To give charters to banks.

These are some examples of prerogatives the expression, "to coin money," does not authorize. If the writers of the Constitution had wanted to give Congress the power to issue notes as media of exchange, they would have used explicit language to express something that had contextual meaning at the time; they would have written "to emit Bills of Credit" after the phrase, "to coin money." That is exactly what they wrote in the Articles of Confederation and in Article I, Section 10, Clause 1 of the Constitution.

Thomas James Norton writes in *The Constitution of the United States—Its Sources and Its Application*, "The Articles of Confederation forbade Congress to borrow money or 'emit bills' unless 'nine States assent to the same.' In the Constitutional Convention the words 'or emit bills,' following the word 'money' in the foregoing clause, were stricken out."

What this tells us is that the writers of the Constitution intentionally did not give Congress the power to issue bills of credit, i.e., unredeemable notes to be used to pay for goods and services.

The passage which reads, "The Congress shall have the power to . . . regulate the Value thereof (of money), and of foreign coin," also requires careful study. It does not tell us how, when, or to what value the coins should be regulated. The Constitution does not instruct Congress "to fix the value thereof." Likewise, it does not direct the Congress "to regulate the alloy thereof." The alloy of a coin is not the exchange value of the coin. The alloy of a coin is the metal substance of the coin. The exchange value of a coin is one's idea of the things for which the coin can be exchanged.

The word "value" by itself has no meaning because there are a number of different values, such as food value, sentimental value, utility value, and exchange value, among others. When we are talking about the amount of goods or services for which coins can be exchanged, we should use the term "exchange value."

The verb "to regulate" means to adjust. And value, in this context, means the exchange value of the coins. So we must determine to what value and, most important, when the exchange value of the coins, including foreign coins, should be adjusted.

The phrase "to regulate the value thereof" cannot mean to regulate, to adjust, or to change the number of grains of metal in the coins because after the coins are made their metal content cannot be changed without destroying them. We know that the value of the foreign coins was regulated without destroying the coins. We know that the exchange value of coins can fluctuate without in any way changing the number of grains of metal in the coins, just as the exchange value of a bushel of wheat can change without adding to or taking away any of the wheat from the bushel.

It may be useful here to review briefly the term, "exchange value." The exchange value of an item is a person's idea of the things for which an item can be exchanged. If I know that I can exchange one bushel of wheat for two bushels of oats, I will say that the exchange value of one bushel of wheat is two bushels of oats. Or I may say that the exchange value of one bushel of oats is one-half bushel of wheat.

If another person has different information, however, and he knows that he can exchange one bushel of wheat for three bushels of oats, he will say the exchange value of one bushel of wheat is three bushels of oats. It is not the bushel of wheat or the bushels of oats that changed, but the exchange value of the wheat and the oats. So we see that the exchange value of an item is a person's idea of the things for which the item can be exchanged.

The same principle applies to gold and silver coins. The writers of the Constitution knew that the exchange value of gold and silver coins changes because they and the rest of the population were using foreign gold and silver coins. There were no United States coins in existence at the time the Constitution was written. Thus the writers of the Constitution had a good reason for stipulating that the value of the coins should be regulated, i.e., adjusted; not fixed.

Therefore, the phrase "to regulate the value thereof" has to mean just what it says, i.e., to regulate or adjust the exchange value (not the metal content) of the coins. The coins remain the same, but the exchange value of the coins will increase or decrease according to the market exchange value of the metal in the coins.

The exchange value of the coins and the number of grains of metal in the coins are two different things. Any regulating or adjusting of the number of grains of metal in the coins can be done only by making new coins. The regulating or adjusting of the exchange value of the existing coins, however, has to be done after the coins are minted.

Because the exchange value of the coins may increase or decrease according to the market value of the metal in the coins, it was proper for the writers of the Constitution to give Congress the power to regulate or adjust the value of the coins to the market value of their metal content after the coins were minted; this was how the value of foreign coins was regulated.

It was the practice of government officials and others to accept for payments due all foreign gold and silver coins and value them for payment purposes according to the market value of their gold or silver content at the time of the transaction.

When we consider the passage in Article I, Section 8, Clause 5, which states "The Congress shall have Power . . . to coin Money, regulate the Value thereof, and of foreign coin . . .," it strongly indicates that the writers of the Constitution wanted Congress to regulate the exchange value of the United States gold and silver coins in the same manner as foreign coins.

It is proper for u' therefore, to conclude that the

writers of the Constitution meant that Congress should have the power to adjust or to regulate the exchange value of the United States gold and silver coins to the market value of their metal content at the time the coins were used as a payment to the government or by the government. That is exactly what the federal government and the states were doing and intended to continue to do with foreign gold and silver coins. Why? Because foreign coins were the only gold or silver coins they had or would have for some time. The idea was practical because it worked. It was just because everyone received what was due him.

How do we know that the legal tender value or the exchange value of the gold or silver coins should be adjusted to the market value of their metal content? If the legal tender value of the coins is adjusted to an amount below the market value of their metal content, people will not use the coins as legal tender. They will hoard the coins or exchange them for the higher market value. If the Congress adjusted the legal tender value above the market value, as was done with silver coins between 1854 and 1964, the coins become token coins. Token coins do not need to be made of silver or gold, as we learned after 1965. The only practical thing for the government to do, therefore, is to adjust the exchange value or the legal tender value of gold and silver coins to the market value of their metal content at the time the coins are presented as a payment or used as a payment.

The Congress on one occasion did regulate the value of the U.S. gold coins in the same manner as foreign coins. It did that in a separate part of the Act of 1834, when it declared that all gold Eagles ($10 gold coins) coined up to that time would have a legal tender value of $10.60, the then current market value of the metal in the coins.

TOKEN COINS

The phrase "to regulate the Value thereof" was not intended to apply to token coins. Token coins are coins with a face value or a legal tender value that is higher than the market value of their metal content. They may or may not contain gold or silver. Token coins are issued as documents. They give certain evidence. Before 1933, they gave evidence that Congress authorized their exchange for gold coins in an amount equal to their face value and they were legal tender for payments up to 25¢ for the one-cent and the five-cent coins and for payments up to $10 for the silver fractional coins. After 1933, the United States token coins were declared to be legal tender for all payments and therefore gave evidence that they would be received by the United States government for any kind of payment at their face value.

So the directive "to regulate the Value thereof" does not apply and never did apply to the United States token coins.

"AND FIX THE STANDARD OF WEIGHTS AND MEASURES"

Now we come to the Constitutional mandate that Congress fix the Standard of Weights and Measures." Note that the word "fix" was used in the language pertaining to standards for weights and measures, but not in the wording covering the coining of money. Article I, Section 8 does not, after granting Congress the power "to coin money," add that Congress should "fix the value thereof." It said that Congress was "to regulate the value thereof." Is that not another reason to deduce that the writers of the Constitution did not intend to give Congress the power to set or fix the exchange value of gold and silver coins? Is it not reasonable to conclude that the Constitution gives the Congress the power only to regulate the exchange value of the United States gold and silver coins in the same manner as the government was doing with the foreign gold and silver coins?

Furthermore, the enjoining of Congress to fix the Standard of Weights and Measurements, did not include the power to fix or establish the exchange value of the gold and silver coins as a "standard of value." The only standards to be fixed were for weights and measurements. Coins are not weights or measurements.

It is true that standard coins were made and all coins were made to conform to those standard coins. Thus, the coins were called standard gold or standard silver coins. But the Constitution did not provide that the gold and silver coins have a standard exchange value. That is, the Constitution did not give Congress the power to declare the amount of goods or services for which the coins can be exchanged.

ARTICLE I, SECTION 10, CLAUSE 1

"No State shall . . . make any thing but gold and silver Coin a Tender in Payment of Debts; . . ."

That clause does not give Congress the right or the power to do anything. That clause does not even give the states the right to declare gold and silver coin to be legal tender. The states already had that right. After the states became independent from England, they had complete sovereignty. They could declare anything to be legal tender and they did declare bills of credit to be legal tender.

However, from their experience with bills of credit, they learned that when anything other than gold or silver coin was declared to be legal tender, injustices occurred. Therefore, when the Constitution was written, that clause was inserted to prohibit the state officials from making anything other than gold or silver coin a legal tender.

CHAPTER XI

THE FRACTIONAL RESERVE BANKING SYSTEM

What is the fractional reserve banking system? Banks are private institutions or corporations established for the purpose of rendering services to the public with the hope of making a profit for the owners (stockholders) of the bank. A commercial bank is a bank that accepts checking accounts. Checking accounts are also called demand deposit accounts. Many people believe that when a commercial bank makes a loan it lends its cash. A commercial bank may lend cash but in practice it seldom does. If a prospective borrower wishes to borrow cash in any quantity, he is apt to be asked to open a checking account and then the banker will enter his loan as a demand deposit in his checking account. Nearly all commercial bank loans are made in that manner. Cash is seldom given to the borrower.

People may believe that the loan is made as a demand deposit for the convenience of the borrower and it is true, of course, that a checking account is convenient for the borrower but with our present shortage of currency (cash), the banks do not have enough currency to make all their loans in currency. There is not enough currency in existence. The main reason for the checking account loan system, however, is that it is the most profitable way for a bank to make loans. If enough currency existed, there would be no need for banks to make loans of bank credit.

As an example, we had on July 1, 1971, about 210 billion dollars' worth of purchasing media in circulation. Of that amount, about 6 billion was in coins and about 50 billion in Federal Reserve notes. The other 154 billion were in the form of demand deposit accounts of bank credit.

Let us give a brief description of how the fractional reserve banking system works in the making of demand deposit loans. The First City Bank has $50,000 worth of currency in its vault. Tom, a local business man, enters the bank and asks for a $10,000 loan. If the bank gave Tom the loan in currency, the bank then would have only $40,000 worth of cash left. But if, instead of giving Tom the $10,000 in cash, the bank had Tom open a checking account and then wrote in his account a bookkeeping entry (a credit) of $10,000 as a demand deposit loan, the bank would thus make the loan and still have the $50,000 worth of cash in the bank. In addition, the bank would now have Tom's $10,000 deposit and Tom's note for $10,000 as an extra asset.

Thus we see that when a commercial bank makes a loan as a demand deposit, it has, after the loan is made, the same amount of cash it had before it made the loan. Also, its assets increased by the amount of the loan.

One may say, yes, but when Tom writes a check to Peter for the $10,000, the bank would have to give Peter the cash when Peter comes in to cash the check. That is true only if Peter asks for the cash. But usually when Peter comes in to cash his check, he does not take out currency. He deposits the $10,000 check in his checking or savings account. The First City Bank then would debit Tom's account by $10,000 and add a $10,000 credit to Peter's account. So, the First City Bank would still have the $50,000 in currency.

Of course Peter might cash and deposit the check at the Second City Bank. In that event, the First City Bank would have to transfer the $10,000 worth of currency to the Second City Bank. But James, a new customer, may come in and deposit a different check for $10,000 made against the Second City Bank. That would bring the $10,000 worth of currency back again. So, in practice, all banks operate nearly as one bank. That is why it is possible for a bank to make loans as demand deposits and still keep its cash.

The above examples show that the checking accounts and the demand deposit loans are not just a convenience, they are needed as a substitute for currency so long as we do not have an adequate supply of currency.

When a loan is made as a demand deposit, that bookkeeping entry represents a claim for currency which is supposed to be in the bank. Usually enough currency is in the bank for each loan at the time the loan is made, but there is seldom enough cash in the bank for all the loans taken as a whole.

Demand deposit accounts are checking accounts. A

check made out by the drawer is an order to the bank to pay currency to the payee of the check. The bank is able to pay currency for such checks only so long as a small percentage of the holders of the checks ask for currency. There is, at the present time, just not enough currency in the country to equal all demand deposit accounts.

Because of the shortage of currency, the banks have adopted the system whereby they make loans as demand deposits (bookkeeping entries) and keep a fraction of the amount of the loan in currency (cash) in the bank as a reserve. Such a banking system is called a fractional reserve banking system. This is the system used in the United States and probably in all other countries as well.

Let us give another example to show in greater detail how the fractional reserve banking system works. Let us suppose that the First City Bank opens up for business with $50,000 worth of currency in its vault. Tom comes in and borrows $10,000. It is given to him as a demand deposit in his checking account. The bank keeps the $50,000 in currency.

Dick comes in and borrows $15,000 in the same manner as Tom did. Harry, too, comes in and borrows $25,000 in the form of a demand deposit, just as Tom and Dick did. The bank has now made loans of $50,000 but it still has the $50,000 worth of cash in its vault.

Now let us have ten other borrowers come in, one at a time, each one borrowing $10,000 in the form of demand deposits.

Another ten borrowers come in consecutively and again each borrows $10,000 in the form of demand deposits.

The bank has now made $250,000 worth of loans, but it still has only the $50,000 in cash in its vault. The $50,000 is the fraction which the bank holds in cash as the reserve for the $250,000 loans made in the form of demand deposits. When we divide the $250,000 into the $50,000 it equals 20%. So this bank would say that it held 20% cash reserves for its demand deposit accounts.

The legal requirements for demand deposits are from 7% to 22%; for time and savings deposits, from 3% to 10%.

If this bank wishes to keep a 20% reserve for its demand deposit accounts, it cannot make any more loans until someone makes a payment or a deposit. But soon a lady enters the bank and deposits $1,000 in a savings account. If the bank's policy requires a 10% reserve for that $1,000 savings account, the bank will set aside $100 of that $1,000 for that reserve. The bank now has $900 which it can use as a 20% reserve for additional demand deposit loans. With that $900 as a 20% reserve, it can make an additional demand deposit loan of $4,500. (20% of $4,500 = $900) That in essence is how the fractional reserve banking system works.

BANK CREDIT

When a bank makes a loan or an investment in the form of a demand deposit, it is considered to be extending bank credit. A student was once asked, "What is bank credit?" He answered, "Bank credit is nothing." Who could say that he was wrong!

To define bank credit we might say that it is a loan or an investment (a bank makes an investment when it purchases a bond) made by a commercial bank, not by giving out any of its cash, but by making a bookkeeping entry as a credit in the payee's demand deposit account.

Bank credit in this form could not exist if the fractional reserve banking system did not exist. Bank credit is a verbal promise by the banker that he will pay out currency on demand. A bank does not and cannot pay out bank credit. A verbal promise cannot be paid out. It is not something to be put in a purse. But a verbal promise can be transferred from one person to another person. That is how bank credit is used as a medium of exchange.

The bookkeeping entries in the demand deposit accounts are the evidence of those verbal promises and they are the evidence of the transfer of those verbal promises.

The bank may and sometimes does pay out currency to fulfill its promises, but in most cases, when a bank is ordered to pay currency to a payee by means of a check, it simply transfers its verbal promise to pay currency to the payee by bookkeeping entries, that is, by debiting the account of the writer of the check and by crediting the account of the payee of the check. The verbal promise is thus transferred from one person to another person.

Under the fractional reserve banking system, the banks have enough currency to fulfill only a fraction of those verbal promises. If a 100% reserve banking system were established for demand deposits, the banks would have enough cash on hand to fulfill all of those verbal promises on demand.

It has been said that money (meaning the purchasing media) will not manage itself. What this really means is that given the fractional reserve banking system, the extension of bank credit (the banks' verbal promises to pay out more cash than they possess) must be managed or controlled.

But who is to control the controllers, especially when their decisions to increase or decrease the money supply are made in secret meetings? The actions of the Federal Reserve Board are not made public until weeks after they have been taken. It should be noted that whoever controls the money supply controls the prices of the goods and services exchanged with that money supply.

In other words, if people wish to be employed in the production, distribution, and exchanging of their goods and services, they will have to raise or lower their prices and wages to correspond to the increase or decrease of the money supply. If, when the money supply is increased, prices and wages are not increased, shortages of goods and services will result. If, when the money supply is decreased, prices and wages are not decreased, unemployment will result. Remember what we learned in chapter VI in the story about Peter Meyer and Count Schlick!

Of course, when every commercial bank in the country can make loans of bank credit simply by making bookkeeping entries in demand deposit accounts, there must be some authority that decides how much bank credit should be extended. The Congress has designated the Federal Reserve Board as that authority. Whatever its merits, the Board has been unable or unwilling to prevent the banking system from extending inflationary bank credit; and it did not prevent the deflation of bank credit and the bank failures in the 1930s. The solution will come only when people learn how to operate demand deposit accounts on a 100% cash reserve basis.

DEMAND DEPOSITS: TWO TYPES

If John Smith earned $1,000 worth of currency and deposits it in his checking account, the bank will call that deposit a demand deposit. The bank received $1,000 worth of currency and is responsible for keeping it and for paying it out when ordered to do so by means of a check. That is one type of demand deposit.

As an example of the second type of demand deposit, John Smith goes to the same bank and asks for a loan of $1,000. The bank gives him the $1,000 loan by making a bookkeeping entry of $1,000 in his checking account. That bookkeeping entry is the other type of demand deposit. Both types of deposits are recorded in the same account. Note that in the second instance the bank did not receive any currency from anyone for that deposit. In fact, the currency for that demand deposit had not yet been earned by anyone. In effect, by giving his note for that demand deposit, John Smith promised to earn $1,000 worth of currency in order to pay for that demand deposit at a later date. Surely, there is a difference between these two types of deposits, but the same term, demand deposit, is applied to both types.

If all deposits were made with currency, or with checks that could be cashed for currency on demand, the banks then would be operating with a 100% reserve banking system. Then there would be only one type of demand deposit. No authority, such as the Federal

Reserve Board, would be needed to control the reserves of the banks.

When we read a bank statement published in a newspaper, we see that the demand deposit accounts are usually several times greater than the cash on hand and the cash due from banks. That tells us the amount the bank has available with which it can pay the depositors of the demand accounts.

Note that we are not including the time and savings deposits as demand deposits because they do not have to be paid on demand.

The bankers may tell us that they can sell some of their bonds to obtain more cash with which to pay their demand deposits. But they cannot sell the bonds unless someone is willing to buy them and has the cash with which to pay for them. If the cash is taken out of another bank, then that bank will have less cash with which to pay its demand depositors.

BANK STATEMENT

The following is a copy of a bank statement given by a bank doing business on October 15, 1974:

BANK STATEMENT

ASSETS

Cash and due from banks	$4,583,043.05
Obligations of Federal Financing Bank	4,054,592.07
Obligations of other U.S. government agencies	698,105.42
Obligations of state and political subdivisions	3,684,605.47
Federal funds sold and securities purchased	400,000.00
Other loans	16,017,841.84
Bank premises and fixtures	1,446,974.58
Other assets	320,211.57
Total Assets	31,205,374.00

LIABILITIES

Demand deposits	11,756,466.61
Time and savings deposits	14,128,543.47
Federal funds purchased and securities sold	1,206,377.36
Mortgage indebtedness	755,768.12
Other liabilities	655,401.07
Total Liabilities	28,502,556.63

RESERVES

Reserves for bad debt losses on loans	272,724.29

CAPITAL ACCOUNTS

Equity capital	2,430,093.08
Total Liabilities, Res. & Cap. Accounts	31,205,374.00

If a bank makes a cash loan for $1,000, the bank statement will show $1,000 less cash after the loan is made than it had before the loan was made. If a bank makes a loan of $1,000 and the bank statement shows the same amount of cash as before the loan was made, the loan was made with bank credit.

Likewise, if a bank records a bookkeeping entry of a demand deposit for $1,000 and, after the bookkeeping entry was made, has no more cash than it had before, the demand deposit was just a bookkeeping entry because no cash was received. The banker pretended that he received cash.

To determine from a bank statement the amount of loans, investments, and demand deposits the bank has made with bank credit (bookkeeping entries), take the data from the bank statement and place the figures in the following categories:

1. The total amount of its loans and investments.
2. The total amount of funds the bank received from all sources.

3. The total amount the bank spent for its premises, fixtures, and other assets.
4. The total amount of its demand deposits.

Now subtract the amount it spent from the amount it received. The result will be the amount available for loans, investments, and to pay out the demand deposit accounts.

Next, subtract from that figure the amount of demand deposits. The balance will be the amount available for loans and investments.

Now subtract that figure from the amount of loans and investments really made. The answer will be the amount of loans and investments made with bank credit (bookkeeping entries).

To prove that the answer is correct, pretend that the bank credit is cash and add it to the amount the bank received and then finish the problem. The result will show that the bank received enough cash to make all the loans and investments with cash and that it also is able to pay out all demand deposits with cash.

Another way to determine from a bank statement the amount of loans, investments, and demand deposits the bank has made with bank credit is as follows:

Subtract the amount under the headings of "cash" and "due from banks" from the amount of demand deposits and multiply by two. The answer will be the amount of loans, investments, and demand deposits made with bank credit.

Because the loans and investments made with bank credit are equal to the demand deposits made with bank credit, all we have to do is to multiply the amount of demand deposits made with bank credit by two to determine the amount of loans, investments, and demand deposits made with bank credit.

In the following worksheet we take the data from the above bank statement and show the arithmetic used to determine from a bank statement the amount of loans, investments, and demand deposits made with bank credit.

BANK STATEMENT WORKSHEET

LOANS AND INVESTMENTS MADE:	
Obligations of Federal Financing Bank	$4,054,592.07
Obligations of other U.S. government agencies	698,105.42
Obligations of state and political subdivisions	3,684,605.47
Federal funds sold and securities purchased	400,000.00
Other loans	16,017,841.84
Total amount of loans and investments made	$24,855,144.80
AMOUNT THE BANK RECEIVED FOR ITS BUSINESS:	
Cash on hand and cash due from banks (from depositors)	4,583,043.05
Capital equity (from stockholders)	2,430,093.08
Reserves (from profits)	272,724.29
Time and savings (from depositors)	14,128,543.47
Federal funds purchased (from banks)	1,206,377.36
Mortgage indebtedness (from borrowings)	755,768.12
Other liabilities (value received from others)	655,401.07
Total amount received for the bank's business	$24,031,950.44

AMOUNT SPENT:	
Bank premises and fixtures	$1,446,974.58
Other assets	320,211.57
Total amount spent	−1,767,186.15
Net amount available for the bank's business	$22,264,764.29
TOTAL DEMAND DEPOSITS (Amount bank must pay on demand)	−11,756,466.61
Net amount available for loans and investments	−10,508,297.68
Demand deposits, loans, and investments made with bank credit	$14,346,847.12

NOTE BELOW: The simple way to obtain the same information.

Demand deposits	$11,756,466.61
Cash on hand and cash due from banks	−4,583,043.05
Amount of demand deposits made with bank credit	7,173,423.56
Multiply by 2	2
Demand deposits, loans, and investments made with bank credit	$14,346,847.12

THE BANK OF ENGLAND

The Bank of England, a privately owned bank established in 1694, was probably the first to make *legal* use of the fractional reserve banking system. Since that time, with the exception of a period between 1842 and the Civil War, when the state banks of Louisiana were required to operate on a 100% reserve system, all commercial banks in the United States have operated on a fractional reserve system.

THE BANK OF AMSTERDAM

The Bank of Amsterdam was established in 1609 by the officials of the City of Amsterdam in Holland. It was established as a 100% reserve banking system, meaning it was always able to pay on demand every depositor's money in gold or silver coins or bullion. It operated for nearly two centuries—181 years—without a failure. It failed in 1790 because it did not stay on the 100% reserve system. In that final year, when the bank could not pay all of its depositors, it was discovered that some years earlier the officers of the bank secretly and illegally loaned a large part of its gold and silver to a private company and to governmental bodies. After those loans were made the bank operated on a fractional reserve system. The bank officers who subsequently took control were honest, but the bank failed because it was on a fractional reserve system. It no longer had the full amount of cash to fulfill its obligations to pay on demand.

We mention the 100% reserve banking system used in Louisiana and Amsterdam in order to point out that a 100% reserve system has worked successfully in the past.

THE CONSEQUENCES OF THE USE OF THE FRACTIONAL RESERVE BANKING SYSTEM

By allowing commercial banks to practice fractional reserve banking, the banks are given the right legally to loan out funds they do not have available for loans. No person and no other corporation are given such a right. Not even the individual owners of the bank have such a right. Yet all the bank owners collectively are given the right legally to loan out funds they do not possess.

The idea of the fractional reserve banking system began in 1694, with the establishment of the Bank of England. Before 1694, individuals would, at times, loan out money they did not own (money they were safe-keeping for others), but when they were caught they were run out of town for their dishonesty.

The following are some of the consequences that result from the use of fractional reserve banking for demand deposits:

IT IS EXTENSIVELY USED

Probably over 90% of all buying and selling in the United States is done with demand deposits of bank credit. The demand deposits are transferred from one person to another by means of written orders (checks) to the bank.

IT IS EXPENSIVE

The fractional reserve banking system provides a convenient, but expensive, means to make up for the shortage of bona fide currency. It provides a legal opportunity for the commercial banks to charge interest on bank credit, even on inflationary bank credit.

IT ALLOWS THE FEDERAL RESERVE SYSTEM TO INFLATE AND DEFLATE THE MONEY SUPPLY.

The individual banker has no way of knowing for certain whether the granting or the refusal to grant a particular loan or the making of a particular investment will cause an increase or decrease of the money supply. The result is that the local bankers and the general public must guess and gamble regarding future economic conditions. Only those who control the fractional reserves for the banking system know what the economic future will be because by controlling the banks' reserves, they control the money supply and create the future economic conditions. Thus, they have a great advantage over all other people. The members of the Federal Open Market Committee of the Federal Reserve System are the ones who exercise the greatest control over the reserves for the banking system.

IT PROVIDES THE MEANS FOR MONETIZING DEBTS

The use of the fractional reserve banking system as a means of creating bank credit "money" requires that the people and/or governmental bodies remain in perpetual and increasing debt. If they do not incur and maintain debts, they have no bank credit "money." If they pay off the debts, they again have no bank credit "money." If they do not pay off the debts, they lose the property they pledged as collateral for the loans. Under the fractional reserve banking system for demand deposits, people are forced into a perpetual round of going in debt, paying off the debt, renewing the debt, and paying interest on the bank credit "money" created by monetizing debts.

We must keep in mind that the "money" made out of debts is not real earned currency. It is not the evidence of a claim for goods or services. It is not a tax credit certificate. It is a substitute for bona fide currency; it is created out of nothing by the making of bookkeeping entries.

IT IS A CAUSE OF BANK FAILURES

Banks operating on a fractional reserve system for demand deposits will always fail when too many depositors try to convert their deposits into currency within a short period of time. When too many depositors are in a rush, when they run to the bank to change their deposits into currency, their action is called a "run on the bank."

Banks operating on a 100% reserve system may fail for other reasons, such as poor management, theft, and embezzlement by officers or employees. That is what happened to the Bank of Amsterdam. But those failures do not take place because of any weakness in the 100% reserve system. The failures occur because of human weaknesses. A bank is said to fail, and it must close its doors, when it is unable to pay its depositors the amount of currency the depositors have a right to claim on demand.

ITS CONSEQUENCES ARE CONCEALED

Problems, such as inflation of the money supply, deflation of the money supply, bank failures, general unemployment, and ever increasing interest-bearing debts by governmental bodies, corporations, and individuals are consequences of the practice of fractional reserve banking for demand deposits. But this is not apparent to the people.

IT IS NOT NECESSARY

Banks operating on a 100% reserve system for demand deposits can charge a fee for servicing their demand deposit accounts. They can loan out their time and savings deposits in the same manner as the savings banks and the savings and loan associations do.

HOW TO CHANGE THE FRACTIONAL RESERVE SYSTEM TO A 100% RESERVE SYSTEM FOR DEMAND DEPOSITS

How can the fractional reserve banking system for demand deposits be changed to a 100% cash reserve system? By cash we mean currency issued by the United States government. The currency may be issued in additional coins in denominations of $5, $10, $20, $50, and $100 or in certificates in lieu of coins. The following is an illustration:

10 10

CERTIFICATE IN LIEU OF COINS
of
THE UNITED STATES OF AMERICA

No.________

For value received, this certificate is receivable at its face value for the payment of all customs, fees, fines, taxes, and other charges due the United States government.

(Signed by) (Signed by)
Treas. of U.S. Sec. of the Treasury

No.

For
TEN DOLLARS

10 10

Note that these certificates are to be considered representations of coins and used as coins. When they are sold by the banks to the public, they will be exchanged for coins, United States notes, Federal Reserve notes or demand deposit accounts. That is why they are issued for value received. If they are used by the U.S. government as payment for goods and services, they will inflate the money supply.

These certificates are documents giving written evidence that they will be received by the government as United States coins.

The certificates are not U.S. notes. They contain no promise to pay. They are not tax credit certificates. No tax should be levied to redeem them because they will not be used as a payment for goods and services when they are introduced into circulation. They will come into circulation by being sold or exchanged for other currency or demand deposits. They will not have to be redeemed in anything. They will stay in circulation just as our present coins stay in circulation.

Remember that all buying and selling is bartering, or exchanging one item for another. So when we buy coins, or certificates in lieu of coins, from the government through the banks with our demand deposit accounts, we are exchanging the demand deposit account for the coins or certificates.

When all demand deposits of bank credit are exchanged for coins and/or certificates in lieu of coins, enough currency will be in circulation so that the banks can have 100% reserves for all demand deposit accounts.

Because the change from fractional reserve banking to 100% reserve banking for demand deposits should take place gradually, we suggest that the government agencies which charter the banks establish a schedule of reserve increase of 20% annually. After one year, for example, demand deposit accounts could be required to have a 20% reserve; after two years, 40%; three years, 60%; four years, 80%, and after five years, 100%. In order to enable the banks to implement this program, the demand depositors must make demand deposits of currency instead of bank credit. This can be done by writing a check to the bank for the amount of the deposit and asking for coins, or certificates in lieu of coins, and then redepositing them in the demand deposit account, with the insistence that the bank keep the total amount as a 100% reserve for the account. The bank and the depositor must agree on a just fee to be paid to the bank for servicing the account.

The time and savings deposits should require the same reserves as those in mutual savings banks and in savings and loan associations, i.e., from zero to three percent. Only demand deposits need 100% reserves. The banks will make their loans and investments from time and savings deposits.

We suggest that no Federal Reserve notes be used for any of the banks' 100% reserves. The Federal Reserve notes are also to be exchanged for coins or certificates in lieu of coins. Thus, they will be returned to the Federal Reserve banks to redeem the government bonds that were deposited as collateral at the time the notes were issued.

Let us suppose there is about 160 billion dollars' worth of demand deposits in the banks, and that approximately 150 billion dollars of it are demand deposits of bank credit. The other 10 billion consists of deposits of existing currency. It is the 150 billion in bank credit that should be exchanged for United States currency. When that is done, enough currency will be in circulation so that banks can operate their demand deposit accounts on a 100% reserve basis. There will be no more purchasing media in circulation than before and, as an additional benefit, the government will make from the sale of the coins and the certificates in lieu of coins a profit of nearly 150 billion dollars which should be used to reduce the debt of the United States government.

WHY IS THE SALE OF THE COINS AND CERTIFICATES SO PROFITABLE?

To simplify the explanation let us use the Eisenhower one-dollar coin as an example. Newspaper reports have stated that it costs the government about six cents to make each Eisenhower dollar coin. The government sells it (deposits it for credit) through the Federal Reserve banks to the local banks and then to the public for one dollar's worth of demand deposits and/or Federal Reserve notes. Thus, it makes a profit of 94 cents on each coin. The profit the government makes in the minting of coins is called seigniorage. The seigniorage for gold coins between 1794 and 1934 was very small as was the seigniorage for silver coins between 1794 and 1873. The seigniorage for our present coins varies from about 6/10 of a cent for the one-cent coin to about 94 cents for the one-dollar coin.

The government declares the one-dollar coin, for which it paid six cents, to be legal tender for a one-dollar payment and it receives the coin for any one dollar payment due the government. That is why the people will pay one dollar for it.

When the government sells or deposits the one-dollar coin for a one-dollar credit in a Federal Reserve bank, it pretends that the coin is equal in exchange value to a coin with one dollar's worth of silver. If the government made a coin with one dollar's worth of silver, it would also sell it for $1 to the Federal Reserve banks. (We assume the coin is not sold for numismatic purposes.)

A coin with a legal tender value of one dollar, containing one dollar's worth of silver, would be received, not redeemed, for any payment of one dollar. It would stay in circulation. It is a full bodied coin. Full bodied coins do not have to be redeemed in anything. They are items with exchange value in themselves which is equal to their market value as a commodity.

When the government declares coins to be legal tender, it pretends that the coins are full bodied coins. It sells them, or receives credit for them, at the same price that it would obtain for full bodied coins. Because the government and the people treat them as full bodied coins, they circulate as full bodied coins. And as long as the government receives them at their face value for payments due it, they will keep their face value for other payments.

Now, if the government issued certificates in lieu of coins, the cost would be much less than for coins. So the profit would be over 99% of the face value of the certificates.

SUMMARY ON THE FRACTIONAL RESERVE BANKING SYSTEM

Banks render useful services. Because of the shortage of bona fide currency, however, they are forced to make loans of bank credit through the use of the unsound fractional reserve banking system. When a bank uses a sysreserves would be needed, no controls by the Federal Reserve System or any other agency would be needed, and no inflation of the money supply would result. The money supply would be in balance with the amount of goods being offered for sale.

CHAPTER XII

THE FEDERAL OPEN MARKET COMMITTEE

The Federal Open Market Committee was created by Congress in 1933 as an amendment to the Federal Reserve Act and is a part of the Federal Reserve System. It is a committee composed of the seven members of the Board of Governors and the presidents of the twelve Federal Reserve banks. However, only five Federal Reserve bank presidents at a time are permitted to be voting members. The voting members are rotated on a regular basis. The president of the New York Federal Reserve bank, however, is a permanent voting member, so actually it is only the other four Federal Reserve presidents who rotate as voting members.

The committee must meet at least four times each year, but it usually meets almost every third Tuesday. It sets the policy to be implemented by the manager of the Open Market Account. The manager, an agent of the Federal Reserve bank of New York, buys and sells the securities for all twelve Federal Reserve banks. Every day this manager buys, sells, and otherwise exchanges securities worth millions of dollars and sometimes more than a billion.

The Annual Report of the Board of Governors for 1970 shows that the value of the Federal Open Market Committee transactions for that year was $110 billion. (Page 73 of Hearings before the Committee on Banking and Currency, House of Representatives, Ninety-third Congress—First Sessions, October 2 and 3, 1973.

A special manager buys and sells foreign currencies and bills but we shall not discuss that aspect of the Committee operations.

The most important function of the Federal Open Market Committee (F.O.M.C.) is to increase or decrease the money supply. It does this by the deliberate and judicious buying and selling of securities on behalf of the twelve Federal Reserve banks.

The F.O.M.C. can, without informing the government, the public, or the banks (its meetings are held in secret), increase or decrease the reserves of the banks. For example, if it wants the money supply to increase, it will buy government securities. If it wants the money supply to decrease, it will sell securities. The Federal Reserve banks can buy an unlimited amount of securities because they do not have to pay for the securities with anything. They pay for the securities by making bookkeeping entries in the member-banks' reserve accounts. They, of course, pay for the securities with a check, but that check is not redeemed with cash. The member bank which cashes the check, instead of receiving cash, receives credit in its reserve account.

Even if the Federal Reserve bank were called upon to pay with currency, an officer could take the U.S. securities, walk to the office of the Federal Reserve agent, who is located in the same building, deposit the securities with him and receive the currency (Federal Reserve notes).

When a bank's reserves are increased, the bank may increase its loans of bank credit from five to ten times its reserves. Thus, the money supply is increased much more than the amount of increase of the reserves.

Because the Federal Reserve banks are not primarily concerned with profit or loss, they can buy securities by bidding up the prices until they obtain the amount they deem necessary. Likewise, they can lower the prices of the securities that they wish to sell until they find a buyer.

The increase or decrease of the price of the securities will cause an increase or decrease of the interest rates on all securities. Thus, the Federal Reserve banks through the the operations of the F.O.M.C. can, without announcing any change in interest rates, cause the interest rates to increase by offering securities for sale at a lower price. Or they can cause a decrease in the interest rates by buying securities at a higher price. The local banks will then merely adjust their rates accordingly.

The F.O.M.C. can thus establish the market price for the government securities and also establish the market rate for interest on those securities. The price and the interest rates on government securities influence the price and the interest rates on all securities.

Let us give an example to show the power of the F.O.M.C. Suppose the government wanted to reduce inflation of the purchasing media by one billion dollars and did so by increasing taxes in the amount of one billion dollars. If the government collected that amount and did not spend it, there would be one billion dollars less purchasing media in circulation.

But if the F.O.M.C. wished, it could offset the action of the government by buying about $100,000,000 worth of securities (assuming the banks were operating on a 10% reserve basis), thus increasing the reserves in the commercial banks by $100,000,000. That would enable the banks to loan out about one billion dollars' worth of additional bank credit. If that amount were loaned out, the money supply would be increased by that amount. That would offset the anti-inflationary effects of the one billion dollars the government collected in taxes.

Or suppose the government wished to increase the money supply by one billion dollars by paying for one billion dollars' worth of its expenses with newly minted coins. If the F.O.M.C. wished, it could sell about $100,000,000 worth of its securities and thereby reduce the reserves of the banks by that amount. That would force the banks to reduce their loans of bank credit by about one billion dollars. That would offset (as far as the money supply is concerned) the effect of the government's action of placing one billion dollars' worth of newly minted coins in circulation.

A comparable incident seems to have taken place in

May, 1975, when the government paid out a rebate check of up to $200 to each individual who paid 1974 U.S. income taxes. And in June, 1975, the government paid $50 to every recipient of Social Security Insurance, Supplemental Security Income or Railroad Retirement annuity or pension payments.

The government officials paid out that money in order to increase the money supply in circulation with the hope that these actions would increase the buying and selling of goods and services and thus create more jobs. One side effect of that action was that the government officials had to incur additional interest-bearing debts in order to make those payments. But what happened?

About July 1, 1975, the prime interest rates began to increase. Between July 1 and August 8, 1975, the prime interest rates increased about one percent, from 6 3/4% on July 1 to 7 3/4% on August 8.

The F.O.M.C. buys and sells securities in secret. It does not tell the public the amount of securities it buys and sells until weeks later. However, the people who understand what makes the interest rates go up or down can deduce what actions the F.O.M.C. has taken.

When the interest rates increased in July, 1975, we could conclude that the F.O.M.C. offered for sale on the open market enough securities to cause the price of the securities to decline. That act caused the interest rates to rise.

We thus witnessed a situation in which government officials incurred an extra interest-bearing debt to increase the money supply in circulation and at almost the same time the F.O.M.C. took action to decrease the money supply.

Interest rates might be expected to rise if too great an amount of U.S. funds is sent to foreign countries. But that did not happen, because the United States had a balance of payments surplus and the exchange value of the U.S. currency increased in relation to the exchange value of some foreign currencies. Both of these occurrences indicated that more U.S. funds came into the United States than were sent out.

These are the reasons why we believe the F.O.M.C. sold more securities than it bought during the month of July, 1975. The result was a decrease in the money supply in circulation and an increase in the interest rates, thus offsetting the actions taken by the government.

It is reasonable to conclude that the Federal Reserve System through the operations of the F.O.M.C. is in a position to control, to a large extent, the economic conditions of the country. Is that desirable? If not, what can be done about it?

The answer, again, is that if the government, in lieu of incurring interest-bearing debts, issued bona fide tax credit certificates and paid these certificates out as currency for its needed goods and services, the result would be the following:

1. There would be no government securities for the F.O.M.C. to buy or sell because there would be no government debts.
2. There would be enough debt-free currency in circulation for a 100% reserve demand deposit banking system.
3. There would be no need for agencies such as the Federal Reserve System and the Federal Open Market Committee to control (to increase or decrease) the reserves of the commercial banks.

CHAPTER XIII

DEBTS

Our money system is such that the people and governmental bodies must incur ever increasing interest-bearing debts. But let us keep in mind that we have a very good system, the private enterprise system, for the production of goods and the rendering of services. It is the money system that we use to facilitate the exchanging of our goods and services that needs correcting. Our money system, the system of making money out of debts, is imposed on our governmental bodies and on our private enterprise system. Our government officials and private individuals must learn how to adopt a money system that does not require the incurring of interest-bearing debts.

The debt money system did not become a legally sanctioned one before 1694. We can learn from history how to change our debt money system into a debt-free and interest-free system.

The following figures taken from the Congressional Record—Senate of June 17, 1974—tells us in graphic terms that our money system places us in ever increasing interest-bearing debts:

	Total Gov't and private debt in Billions	Total per capita debt
1929	$215.2	$ 1,757
1949	$510.8	$ 3,393
1969	$1,981.3	$ 9,719
1973	$2,885.6	$13,741

This total interest-bearing debt of more than 2 trillion, 885 billion dollars is now increasing at the rate of more than $9,325 every second. Is it not time to do a little homework?

A debt is an obligation to pay. It is only individuals who can pay debts with their goods and services. A debt made by government officials is an obligation upon the people who pay taxes to that government. A debt made by the officials of a corporation is an obligation placed upon the people who are the stockholders of the corporation. A debt made by the officials of a church congregation is an obligation placed upon the members of the congregation. We may speak of a government debt, a company debt, or a church debt, but all such debts are debts on the individuals within these entities.

People can pay their debts only by their labor or with the product of their labor. So contracts or agreements to pay debts ought to be made so that the debts could be paid with a person's labor (his services) or with the product of his labor (his goods).

Contracts, or agreements to pay, should not be made so that a person has to make his payments with the products of someone else's labor. A man who produces cotton should not agree to make payments with wool, or with copper, or with gold. The man who has sheep can make payments with wool. The man who owns copper can make payments with copper. And the man who owns gold can make payments with gold.

People who own gold, silver, wool, copper or other commodities or merchandise could issue certificates of credit for those items. They could make their payments with those certificates. The commodities and the merchandise would be transferred to the bearer of those certificates on demand. If those certificates were written so that they could be redeemed for cash after a specific date, they would serve as an acceptable currency.

The adoption of such a system would make it convenient and practical for many people to avoid incurring interest-bearing debts. It would enable them to buy other goods and services with the products of their own labor, instead of with the product of someone else's labor. Legal tender and bank credit are not products that can be created by the producers of goods and services. Ultimately, all payments are made with goods or services, even those made with legal tender, because eventually the legal tender is exchanged for goods or services. Whenever it is practical, certificates of credit should be used as a means of making payments and avoiding incurring interest-bearing debts.

Certificates of credit do have some limitations on their acceptability, but that does not mean they should not be used within their limitations. (Personal checks have limitations, yet people use them all the time.)

Certificates of credit issued in lieu of borrowing by a large utility company could serve in a limited way as a practical debt-free medium of exchange and at the same time save the issuing company large interest payments.

The certificates should be issued in convenient denominations in an amount not to exceed the amount of the company's charges for services to its customers. Then those certificates can be used as payments to its employees for wages and salaries. Every certificate would be redeemable either as a payment for the company's services or after a certain date for cash. That is why they would be acceptable as a medium of exchange. The following is an example:

10 10

CERTIFICATE OF CREDIT
of
THE STATE UTILITY COMPANY

No.______ Date______

This certificate is receivable, at its face value, for the payment of all utility bills due The State Utility Company.

Sixty days after date of issue it is redeemable for cash at any office where payments for our utility bills are received.

(Signed by)
Company Treasurer

For
TEN DOLLARS

10 10

When certificates of credit are issued so that they may be redeemed for goods or services on demand and also redeemed for cash after a specific date, they can serve as an acceptable medium of exchange. Because most of our buying and selling is done locally, it is not necessary to use nationally acceptable media of exchange for local transactions. Personal checks serve very well locally, but not so well nationally, yet we still use them in large quantities.

NATIONALLY ACCEPTABLE CERTIFICATES OF CREDIT

To make certificates of credit acceptable nationally, we could have them warranted by nationally recognized corporations for a small fee as we now do when we have checks certified, titles to land insured, the payment of mortgages and leases guaranteed, and the repayment of bank deposits insured by the Federal Deposit Insurance Corporation (FDIC). Such a fee would be small compared to the interest payments required when the currency is borrowed.

Private corporations, like governmental bodies, can avoid incurring interest-bearing debts by the issuing of certificates of credit when it is practical to do so.

INVOLUNTARY DEBT

A person may place himself in debt voluntarily or he may be placed involuntarily in debt by others. An involuntary debt is a debt placed upon a person without his consent by one or more other persons. Generally speaking, an involuntary debt is placed upon people by a governmental body. The issuing of long term government bonds may place an involuntary debt even upon persons not yet born. In addition to the debt itself, interest charges on the debt are placed upon individuals without their consent.

Debts can only be paid with the goods or services of people who do productive work. When individuals are involuntarily made to pay debts, it means that they are forced to work to pay the debts. The term which can appropriately be applied in such cases is "involuntary servitude."

In a country where people decide many issues by voting, those who vote to place other people in debt ought to question whether they have such a right.

Thomas Jefferson once said that the act of placing a debt on our children is tantamount to enslaving them. We believe that most parents would not consider that they have the right to place their children in debt or in slavery. If parents do not have that right then neither do government officials.

The conclusion we draw is that even when government officials believe that debts are worth incurring in order to benefit the people, they have no right to place interest-bearing debts on them unless every person who is obligated to pay those debts gives his consent.

The most important thing to remember, however, is that there is no need for a governmental body to incur an interest-bearing debt. Bona fide tax credit certificates can be issued in lieu of borrowing; then no interest-bearing debt will be needed.

Article I, Section 8 of the United States Constitution states "The Congress shall have the power . . . To borrow money [not bank credit]." That section makes it legal for Congress to place people in debt, but that does not make it necessary or right.

VOLUNTARY DEBT

If a person places himself in debt voluntarily, he places himself in voluntary servitude. He is a bound man. Sometimes he is called a bondman. The person to whom he is bound is called the bondholder. The bondman signs an agreement giving evidence that he binds himself to make a certain payment. This document is called a bond or a note. It is given to the person to whom the bondman is obligated to make the payments. The bondman can become a free man when he fulfills the obligations to which he agreed.

MONETIZING DEBTS

The word "monetize" originally meant to make into coins. Our banking system uses a debt as a substitute for coins.

When the United States government borrows from the

banks, the banks in exchange for bills, notes or bonds, enter these debts as a bookkeeping credit in the amount of the loan in the account of the United States Treasury. That deposit is treated as if the deposit were made with coins. That is a government debt that is monetized.

If a commercial bank makes a loan of bank credit to a person or a private corporation, it does so by making a bookkeeping entry credit in the borrower's checking account. The result is that checks may be written against that account in the same manner as they would be if coins were deposited in that account. In that case a private debt is monetized.

All these debts are monetized because of the scarcity of bona fide currency. If people would learn how to issue and use bona fide debt-free and interest-free tax credit certificates and, if necessary, bona fide debt-free and interest-free certificates of credit, we would have enough non-inflationary currency so that there would be no need or excuse for monetizing debts in order to obtain the needed media of exchange.

GOVERNMENT DEBTS

It is interesting to read various statements regarding government debts. Before 1915, when the United States was in debt to foreign countries, it was said that it was a benefit to the American people to be in debt to foreigners. Now that the United States government debt is held mostly by Americans, some of our textbooks say that as long as the debt is not held by foreigners, the debt is no serious problem, implying that only foreign debts are a serious problem.

The thought must occur to some of us that if a foreign debt is bad for the people of a country, why are we told that we are helping a poor country by making loans to it and thus placing it in debt?

WE OWE IT TO OURSELVES

Some textbooks postulate that as long as we owe the government debts to ourselves, we are not obligated to pay the interest by shipping our goods or services outside of the country. As the payment of interest, or any payment is made with goods and services, the goods and services are paid to ourselves. The implication is that such payments are no burden because we ourselves have the use of these goods and services. Let us study this hypothesis a little further.

It requires work, the expenditure of human energy by individuals to produce goods and services. Now, if the people who work to produce the goods and services that serve as interest payments on the debt were the ones who benefited from these "payments to ourselves," then they could agree that we are paying interest to ourselves. In fact the interest payments could be canceled and no one would complain. We know, however, that the national debt does not offer any such options. If the government stopped paying interest on its debt, we would soon learn who the "ourselves" are. Only the persons who own government securities and receive the interest payments on those securities can say that the interest is paid to "ourselves." They are not speaking for the people who are making the payments.

GOVERNMENTAL BODIES NEED NOT GO IN DEBT

How can a governmental body obtain the currency it needs without borrowing it? All of us, especially government officials, should have the answer to that question. All of us, also, ought to know the end result, if borrowing is the only means used to obtain our media of exchange. When a currency is brought into circulation by borrowing it with interest, the principal with the interest can never be repaid. (See *Money–Bona Fide or Non-Bona Fide*, pages 52 to 56.)

There is a proven method for governmental bodies to obtain their needed currency without incurring interest-bearing debts. In chapter VII we learned that the government of England issued tallies and used them as currency from 1100 A.D. to 1694. Think of it! For 594 years the English government issued currency without going into debt and without paying interest for the use of it.

Now, of course, a governmental body does not have to issue tally sticks, but it can issue tax credit certificates which will serve the purpose even better because they will be just as convenient, just as valuable, and just as acceptable as our present currency.

GOVERNMENT DEBTS ARE USED TO CONTROL THE ECONOMY

The United States government issues bonds, notes, and bills as evidence of its debts. These documents are called government securities. The Federal Reserve banks through the F.O.M.C. buy and sell these securities for the purpose of controlling the reserves of the banking system. The reserves control the supply of bank credit, and the amount of bank credit that can be loaned out controls the economy. A controlled economy is not a free economy.

Thus, we see that when government officials incur a government debt, they give the Federal Reserve System the opportunity to control the economy. As a result of the government debt the taxpayers—the producers and distributors of our goods and services—not only have a heavy burden of interest payments, but they also have to produce and distribute their goods and services with media of exchange controlled by others. Futhermore, the media of exchange (the money supply) is poorly controlled, otherwise, we would not have so many "money" problems.

THERE IS A WAY OUT

The goal must be to pay off the debt and then operate the government without a debt. Any candidate for public office who does not know how to do that should be willing to learn how, or at least be open to suggestions from the people he serves. Only then can he consider himself qualified for a government position.

HOW TO PAY OFF THE DEBT OF THE UNITED STATES GOVERNMENT

To pay off the government debt, Congress must first stop borrowing. When the government needs currency, it should issue bona fide tax credit certificates. Needed goods and services would be purchased with those certificates, a tax levied equal to the amount of the certificates issued, and the certificates received as any payments due the government and redeemed when presented as payment for the taxes which were levied at the time the certificates were issued.

From the time the certificates are issued until they are redeemed, the people would use them as currency. They would have the same value and be just as acceptable as the present coins, United States notes and Federal Reserve notes. The reason our present currency has exchange value—the reason people accept it and use it as currency—is because the government receives it as payment for all charges due the government.

The next step would be for the Congress to carry out the suggestions given in chapter XI which tells how to change the fractional reserve banking systems for demand deposits into a 100% cash reserve banking system for demand deposit accounts.

The government's issuing and selling enough coins and/or certificates in lieu of coins so that the commercial banks can operate their demand deposit accounts on a 100% reserve system would give the government a profit of about 150 billion dollars. That profit would be applied to reduce the debt.

Then the government would issue enough additional coins and/or certificates in lieu of coins, deposit them in the Federal Reserve banks for credit and exchange that credit for the Federal Reserve notes in circulation; then the Federal Reserve notes would be exchanged for the U.S. securities held as collateral for those notes. Those notes would then be canceled and destroyed and the government debts represented by those securities would be paid off. Thus the U.S. government debt would be reduced by another 50 or more billion dollars. This can be done gradually, over a period of about five years.

The two steps outlined above would reduce the debt by about 200 billion dollars. The interest alone saved from those reductions may be about 10 billion dollars annually.

After the 200 billion dollars' worth of the debts is paid off with the profit resulting from the sale of coins and/or certificates in lieu of coins, the remaining portion can be paid off with taxes, but without the need to impose additional taxes.

Because the government would save about 10 billion dollars annually in interest costs as a result of the 200 billion-dollar reduction in the debt, the government can levy a tax of 10 billion dollars annually which otherwise would have gone for interest payments and use that amount to reduce the remaining debts. If that is done for about 25 years, the balance of the debts can be paid off.

If the government would pay off about 200 billion dollars' worth of its debt by the issuing and selling of coins and/or certificates in lieu of coins, would that not cause an inflation of the purchasing media in circulation?

It would if it were not done properly. It is necessary to reduce the dollars' worth of bank credit or Federal Reserve notes in circulation at the same rate the coins and/or certificates in lieu of coins are placed into circulation.

To illustrate, let us suppose that we have 210 billion dollars' worth of purchasing media in circulation. It consists of the following:

United States coins and notes	6 billion
Federal Reserve notes	54 "
Bank credit (demand deposits)	150 "
Total	210 billion

Now let us assume that every person who had Federal Reserve notes went to his bank and exchanged the notes for coins and/or certificates in lieu of coins. The bank would return the Federal Reserve notes to the Federal Reserve bank where they would be returned to the

Federal Reserve agent in exchange for the proper dollars' worth of government bonds which he was holding as security for those Federal Reserve notes. The government then would pay off those bonds with the profit it received from the sale of the coins and certificates in lieu of coins.

If everyone, including the banks, exchanged their Federal Reserve notes for coins or certificates in lieu of coins, the 54 billion dollars' worth of Federal Reserve notes would be out of circulation and 54 billion dollars' worth of new currency would be in circulation. The total amount of purchasing media in circulation would be no more and no less than before.

The profit that the government made from the selling of those new coins and certificates would show up as a credit in the goverment's accounts in the Federal Reserve banks. That credit *must* be used to buy back the government securities held by the Federal Reserve banks. The Federal Reserve banks would merely debit the account in exchange for the bonds. The result would be no increase in the amount of purchasing media in circulation.

On the other hand, if the government used the profit it made from the sale of the coins and certificates in lieu of coins to buy securities from any other source, or if the government used that profit to make payments for any other purpose, an increase of bank reserves would take place. The result would be an inflationary increase of the purchasing media in circulation.

Now let us show how the 150 billion dollars' worth of bank credit which people hold in their demand deposit accounts can be exchanged for coins or certificates in lieu of coins. A person who has a demand deposit of bank credit for $1,000 would write a check for $1,000 payable to the bank which has his checking account and use that check to buy from the bank $1,000 worth of coins or certificates in lieu of coins. That person then will have his $1,000 worth of purchasing media in currency instead of in the form of bank credit. The total amount of purchasing media in circulation will be no more and no less than before.

In order for the bank to replenish its stock of currency (coins and/or certificates in lieu of coins), its officers would send to its Federal Reserve bank a $1,000 check or a $1,000 security and exchange it for $1,000 worth of currency.

In order for the Federal Reserve bank to replenish its stock of currency, the United States treasury would deposit $1,000 worth of new currency in the Federal Reserve bank. The Federal Reserve bank would give the government a credit of $1,000 in its account. With that credit the government must buy back a $1,000 U.S. security from the Federal Reserve bank. The Federal Reserve bank on its part would debit the government account by $1,000 and return the security to the government.

By following that procedure there would be no increase or decrease of purchasing media in circulation and $1,000 worth of government debt would be paid off.

Our purpose here is only to show how to accomplish the exchanges. We have not included the cost of making the coins or printing the certificates in lieu of coins.

It must be emphasized again that the government profit or credit made from the sale of its coins or certificates must be used to buy back its securities from the banking system. If the government spent that credit or profit for any other purpose, the purchasing media in circulation would be increased.

If every person and corporation with demand deposits of bank credit exchanged those deposits for currency, in time, the whole 150 billion dollars' worth of bank credit deposits would be exchanged for 150 billion dollars' worth of currency. The banks then would be on a 100% reserve system for its demand deposit accounts.

In the plan given above, the people and the corporations that exchange their demand deposits of bank credit for currency would not return the currency to the banks. If they did, there would follow a serious inflation of the money supply unless the banking system increased their reserve requirements at the same rate as the new currency was deposited.

How can all that new currency be deposited in the demand deposit accounts so that the depositors can use checks in the payment of their expenses without causing an inflation of the money supply?

That can be done in a just and convenient manner by simply requiring that the banking system adopt the policy of having 100% reserves in currency for all demand deposit accounts. When that is done, everyone can deposit as much of his currency as he wishes in his checking account and then he can pay all of his bills with checks in the normal manner.

A slightly different but practical way to exchange the demand deposits of bank credit into currency would be to require that all reserves be in currency and that the banking system increase over a period of five years their required reserves for their demand deposits, as indicated in chapter XI. During that time, the demand deposits of bank credit would be gradually exchanged for new currency. The system of using checks in the payment of bills would then not be interrupted.

It is necessary that the required reserves for the banking system be increased at the same rate that the deposits of bank credit are exchanged for the deposits of the new currency so that the banking system would not use the newly acquired currency as reserves with which to loan out additional bank credit.

When the whole 150 billion dollars' worth of bank credit deposits are exhanged for coins and certificates in lieu of coins, the banking system will be on a 100% reserve system for demand deposits, i.e., all demand deposits can be paid with currency on demand; and the federal debt will be greatly reduced.

The purchasing media in circulation will then consist of the following:

United States currency	210 billions
Federal Reserve notes	000 "
Bank credit	000 "
Total	210 billions

There would be an increase in the amount of currency in circulation, but there would be no increase in the total dollars' worth of purchasing media in circulation. So there would be no inflation of the money supply or purchasing media in circulation.

THE RESULTS

If the above suggestions were followed in regard to the paying off of the United States government debt, we could expect the following results:

1. In time the U.S. government would be out of debt.
2. The F.O.M.C. would have no services to perform.
3. The Federal Reserve banks would not be needed to:
   (a) supply reserves to commerical banks
   (b) control the banks' reserves
   (c) issue Federal Reserve notes
4. The commercial banks would never fail because of a lack of sufficient reserves.
5. The banking system would have no opportunity to legally issue inflationary purchasing media.
6. There would be enough currency in circulation so that the private enterprise system and governmental bodies would be free from a managed money system.
7. The people would be free from the burden of paying interest on the U.S. government debt.
8. The government officials would be free of the influence of those who formerly controlled the money supply.

SUGGESTIONS FOR A PEOPLE WHO WISH TO BE DEBT FREE

Let us suppose that the people in a state or a country decided to live free from any interest-bearing debts. Whom could they consult in order to obtain the necessary information to carry out their plan? Which college professor would teach them. In answer to this question, one economics teacher said his job was to teach how our economic system works, not to set up such a system. The money and banking courses teach students how the banking system supplies bank credit with interest, mentioning, of course, that people and governments must go into debt to obtain it. So people who wish to live free from debts will have to devise their own plan.

Let us consider some suggestions. The first step would be for the people to refrain from incurring any interest-bearing debts. The second step would be to obtain their media of exchange without borrowing it. If governmental bodies need media of exchange with which to pay for goods and services, they can issue tax credit certificates. The following is a sample copy:

> 10 10
>
> Tax Credit Certificate
> of
> THE STATE OF WISCONSIN
>
> No.______ Date______
>
> This certificate is receivable, at its face value, for the payment of all taxes, fees, fines, and other charges due the State of Wisconsin.
>
> It is redeemable in the payment of taxes due the State of Wisconsin on April 15, 19__. After April 15, 19__, it will be redeemed for cash by the State Treasurer.
>
> (Signed by)
> State Treasurer
>
> For
> TEN DOLLARS
>
> 10 10

Private corporations offering goods, commodites, or products for sale can issue certificates of credit and use them as payments for their needed goods and services. The following is a sample copy:

10 10

Certificate of Credit
of
THE BLANK CORPORATION

No.______ Date______

Within one year after date this certificate is redeemable at its face value for any of the products, goods, or services being offered for sale by the Blank Corporation, or for cash by its treasurer.

(Signed by)
Corporation Treas.

For
TEN DOLLARS

10 10

The above certificates can serve as currency for everyone. Those certificates are valuable because they are redeemable. Tax credit certificates are redeemable when presented as payment for taxes. Certificates of credit are redeemable for the goods or services for which they are the evidence of a claim. Also, under certain conditions, they are redeemable for cash. For example, if the blank corporation has sold all the goods it had for sale, it will have the cash from those sales to redeem any unredeemed certificates with that cash.

Those who possess gold and wish to exchange their gold for other items can issue certificates of credit redeemable in gold. Those who posses silver can issue certificates of credit redeemable in silver. Those who possess other commodities and goods can issue certificates of credit redeemable with the commodities or goods they possess.

Mail order companies can issue certificates of credit redeemable for any of the items listed in their catalogs or offered for sale in their stores. Department stores can pay for at least some of their goods and services with their certificates of credit. The oil companies can issue certificates of credit which would be redeemable for any of their products or services at any of their service stations.

All the issuers of these certificates of credit would issue them as payment for the goods and services they needed and wanted. Those who received them as payment, such as their employees, would, in turn, use them as currency with which to buy the goods and services they wanted. Even governmental bodies could receive them as payments due and in turn use them as currency with which to pay for their needed goods and services.

The banks would be in a position to render for a fee a useful service by receiving, keeping, exchanging, transferring, and paying out these certificates.

LET US BUY A HOUSE WITHOUT INCURRING A DEBT

A couple named Ed and Edith wish to buy a house worth $40,000. They have only $8,000 worth of currency. But Bill, an officer of a local savings and loan association tells them his company has $32,000 worth of surplus funds. Ed and Edith will not borrow the $32,000, but they still would like to buy the $40,000 house. They express their wishes to Bill, who says, "Let me think about it."

The next day Bill calls Ed and suggests the following: "We can build the house together. You pay $8,000 and our savings and loan association will pay the $32,000. You will own one-fifth of the house and we will own four fifths. We will share with you proportionately the cost of all repairs, upkeep, and taxes. You may live in the house by paying a fair rent for our four-fifths share. You will not be in debt to us for the four fifths part we own. We shall agree to sell to you our portion of the house at a mutually agreeable price (the market price) in $2,000 amounts at any time such payments are convenient to you. The rent will be reduced proportionately each time you make a $2,000 payment. You also are free to sell your share of the house at any time for any price you can obtain. Because the buyer will be our tenant, however, he must be a person acceptable to us."

In that manner Ed and Edith obtained a house without going into debt and Bill's savings and loan association made an income producing investment.

START A BUSINESS WITHOUT GOING INTO DEBT

A person who may wish to start a business without incurring a debt may either form a partnership or a corporation with the persons from whom he might otherwise borrow. He would not be in debt to them. They would share his responsibilities, profits, or losses. Bond holders do not share responsibilities, profits, or losses. Many companies have been started in that manner. The point is that there are ways to start a business without incurring interest-bearing debts.

BUILD A CHURCH WITHOUT GOING INTO DEBT

If a congregation wants to build a church before its members are able to pay the total cost, they can do it in the same manner that Ed and Edith obtained their house. The investment company that would normally make a loan to the congregation in exchange for interest-bearing bonds, might be willing to pay for the church and then rent the building to the congregation under the same plan that Bill's savings and loan association formulated for Ed and Edith.

OBTAIN PERSONAL PROPERTY WITHOUT DEBT

Automobiles, farm machinery, household furniture, and many other items are now available by renting or leasing them.

THERE ARE TWO TYPES OF INVESTMENTS

1. Investments in property
2. Investments in debts

What is the difference? When a person invests in property, he is responsible for the care of the property, the payment of taxes, and the production of an income from the property. To accomplish this, he must do the necessary work or hire others to do it. His energy is used to produce goods or services which are always shared with others. Other people are benefited by his labor.

When a person invests in other people's debts, such as bonds and notes (evidence of debts), only the person who incurrs the debt assumes the responsibility for the care of the property, the payment of taxes, the production of an income from the property, and in addition the payment of the interest on the debts.

WHAT IF THERE WERE NO INVESTMENTS TO BE MADE IN DEBTS?

People could invest in property, in stocks, or in savings and loans associations. Savings and loan associations pay dividends, not interest, to their depositors.

BANKRUPTCY WOULD BE ENDED

If people became accustomed to living without debt, no one would ever go bankrupt. A person cannot go bankrupt unless he first goes into debt.

THE BANK OF NORTH DAKOTA

The people of North Dakota have a state banking system which enables them to be somewhat independent when their governmental bodies need loans. The state has its own bank, the Bank of North Dakota. While the Bank of North Dakota does not make loans without charging interest, in practice it does so in part. Much of the interest it receives from its loans is given to the state, thus reducing some of the need for state taxation. So the borrowers are paying interest in lieu of taxes for the support of the state government.

A policy could be adopted so that the profit, after the expenses of operating the bank were paid, would be returned to the borrowers instead of being paid to the state. The borrowers who paid the interest then could say, correctly, we are paying the interest to ourselves. The results would be about the same to them as if they did not pay the interest.

The people of North Dakota could go one step further toward having all governmental bodies in the state free from the burden of interest-bearing debts by doing the following:

The Bank of North Dakota could, with only minor changes of its policy, establish the practice of operating on a 100% bank credit system. It would not receive or pay out any cash. It would make loans of bank credit by issuing checks on itself and it would receive payments only in checks from banks that had accounts in its bank. It would redeem (not cash) its own checks by giving credit in the amount of the checks to the banks that presented them for payment. It would be a completely cashless bank. Let us illustrate with an example:

Let us say the City of Fargo wishes to borrow $1,000,000 from the Bank of North Dakota. The City of Fargo would issue $1,000,000 worth of bonds or notes payable to the Bank of North Dakota over a period of five years. $200,000 of the loan is to be paid back at the end of each of the five years. No interest would be charged, only a service fee sufficient to cover the cost of making and servicing the loan. Perhaps this would be a flat fee of 1%, or an annual fee of $2,000, also payable at the end of each of the five years.

The City of Fargo, on its part, must levy an unrevocable tax of $202,000 for each of those five years in order to make payments. The Bank of North Dakota would then issue a check of $1,000,000 payable to the City of

Fargo. The City of Fargo would deposit the check in its demand deposit account at the Fargo Local Bank and receive $1,000,000 worth of bank credit. The Fargo Local Bank would then send the check back to the Bank of North Dakota and receive $1,000,000 worth of bank credit in its account there.

The City of Fargo would then issue checks against its account up to $1,000,000. The persons receiving the checks would deposit them in any bank and receive credit in their accounts. They in turn would write out checks against their accounts. Thus by having everyone use checks in lieu of cash as their medium of exchange, buying and selling would take place in the usual manner.

At taxpaying time, the people would pay their taxes with checks to the City of Fargo. The City of Fargo would deposit those checks in its Fargo Local Bank and receive credit for them.

At the end of each year when the payments on the bonds are due, the City of Fargo would issue a check for the amount due and send it to the Bank of North Dakota. The Bank of North Dakota would credit the City of Fargo for the amount paid and debit the Fargo Local Bank for that amount and return the endorsed check to the Fargo Local Bank which would debit the City of Fargo's account and return the canceled check to the city treasurer.

That procedure would be repeated at the end of each of the five years, at which time the principal would be repaid without any interest charges. The bank's cost of operations would be taken care of by the 1% service charge; but that is not 1% per year.

It would not be necessary for the Bank of North Dakota to charge any interest on its loans because it would not loan out any cash. It would only loan out bank credit and the bank would not have to pay any interest to obtain that bank credit. The only income the Bank of North Dakota would need is the amount necessary to pay the total cost of its services. It would obtain that amount from the 1% fee.

This suggested system of operating a state bank on a

100% bank credit system is similar to the system practiced by the Federal Reserve banks. The Federal Reserve banks write checks against no funds when they buy securities through the Federal Open Market Committee. Because the Bank of North Dakota acts as the clearing bank for the commercial banks in the state, it, too, could do the same.

The Bank of North Dakota would not make a profit and it should not sustain a loss. The bank would be run to perform a service to the political subdivisions and agencies of the state, so that they could operate without the burden of interest-bearing debts. The commercial banks could continue to make their loans to private corporations and individuals for a profit.

While this system of borrowing interest-free bank credit would be less burdensome for the taxpayers than obtaining interest-bearing loans, still a debt would be incurred. If the taxpayers failed to pay the total amount of the taxes levied on time, the city could not repay the loan. It would be in default.

Whereas, if the city issued bona fide tax credit certificates in lieu of borrowing the bank credit and some people did not pay their taxes on time, the city would not be in default to anyone because the city had incurred no debt to anyone. Only the taxpayers who had not paid their taxes would be in default. No bank would be involved.

CHAPTER XIV

THE DEVALUATION OF THE DOLLAR

Let us try to explain what "devaluation of the dollar" really means. Actually, the word "currency" should be used in place of the word "dollar." The word "dollar" is the name of the unit we use to express the exchange value of our currency as well as the exchange value of goods and services. The unit, dollar, has no exchange value by itself because it is not a physical thing. It is our currency which has exchange value. Our coins, our United States notes, and our Federal Reserve notes may increase or decrease in exchange value. We do not use dollars as our medium of exchange. We use dollars worth of our currency as our medium of exchange.

Thus, when people speak of a devaluation of the dollar, keep in mind that it is the currency, the exchange value of which is expressed in dollars, that has decreased in exchange value. That exchange value may be less only when it is exchanged for gold. But since our currency is no longer based on gold, it now usually means that our currency has less exchange value when it is exchanged for currencies of other countries.

In the past the word "devaluation" was officially used when the government declared that it would refuse to accept its currency in exchange for gold or that it would accept its currency for gold at a lower exchange value. Another way for the government to say the same thing was to declare that the price of gold was increased.

NIXON ANNOUNCES DEVALUATION

On Sunday August 15, 1971, President Richard M. Nixon announced, among other things, that the United States government would no longer exchange foreign held dollars (meaning United States currency) for gold. He said the dollar (meaning United States currency), would be allowed to seek or find its own level. The expression, "we shall let the dollar float," was used.

He, in effect, was admitting that when the United States government was exchanging one ounce of gold for each $35 worth of foreign held United States currency, those who held the currency received the gold at a price which was below the world market price.

And when he said that the dollar would seek or find its

own level, it meant that the people who held United States currency in foreign countries could exchange that currency for any other currencies, goods, or services at any rate of exchange they could obtain for it, just as the people in the United States have been doing since 1934. They would be expected to exchange it for the best offer made to them. That is what is meant by the statement that the dollar, meaning the currency, will float or find its own level. The currency could be exchanged for anything, except gold, being offered for sale in the United States at the same rates the residents of the United States receive when they exchange their currency for goods and services.

THE CAUSE OF NIXON'S ANNOUNCEMENT

In 1934 the United States government promised all non-United States residents that it would exchange (buy or sell) 1/35 of an ounce of gold for each one dollar's worth of United States currency.

By virtue of that promise the United States government gave two exchange values to its currency: One was the general legal tender exchange value given to the currency when it was held by residents of the United States; the other was the additional specific exchange value given to the currency when it was held by non-residents who could exchange each dollar's worth of currency for 1/35 of an ounce of gold.

When a currency has two exchange values, we can expect that the people who possess it will exchange it for the higher value. That is what they did. For a number of years after 1934, very little foreign held United States currency was exchanged for United States gold. Because the price of gold was previously $20.67 per ounce, few were interested in buying it for $35 per ounce. People who bought it for $20.67 were happy to sell it back to the United States for $35. The result was that the United States acquired a large stock of gold.

Beginning about the 1955, however, the price of goods and services, other than gold, increased to such an extent that gold at $35 per ounce became a bargain. In fact, many foreign bankers preferred to exchange their United States currency for gold because gold was their best buy.

Foreign bankers or speculators who owned gold probably believed that the United States government would, in time, raise the price of gold. Therefore, if they could buy the gold at $35 per ounce and later sell it back to the United States for a higher price, they would make an easy profit. But when the world market price was already above our $35 per ounce price, we could no longer sell it for that price.

Because the price of a large percentage of our goods was higher than what the foreigners were willing to pay; because we could no longer sell gold at $35 per ounce; and because foreign bankers held billions of dollars' worth of United States currency for which they still could legally claim gold at $35 per ounce, President Nixon rescinded the 1934 declaration that foreign held U.S. currency could be exchanged for gold at $35 per ounce.

The result was that after August 15, 1971, United States currency held outside of the United States lost one of its exchange values. That is, it lost the exchange value it had as evidence of a claim for gold at $35 per ounce. That is the only exchange value it lost—the same exchange value the currency lost for the residents of the United States in 1934 when President Roosevelt announced that the currency would be exchanged for gold only when it was presented for exchange by foreigners.

After August 15, 1971, the United States currency held by non-United States residents still had all its other exchange values: the currency could be exchanged for stocks, bonds or any other goods or services being offered for sale in the United States.

ARBITRAGE

When international money changers in different countries set a price (rate of exchange) on currencies that are used in international payments, sometimes a currency is given two different exchange value at the same time. When that occurs, speculators attempt to make unearned gains. Such a practice is called arbitrage.

Arbitrage is the simultaneous buying and selling of a foreign currency in the same or different market in order to make a profit. It is usually practiced by large banks and foreign exchange dealers.

CHAPTER XV
QUESTIONS AND ANSWERS

WHY DID THE U.S. GOVERNMENT BUY GOLD?

The buying of gold by the federal government increases the money supply. Let us explain. When the government bought gold, it did not actually "buy" it because it did not tax the people to obtain currency with which to pay for the gold. It merely changed the gold into the current money supply, thereby increasing the money supply. Thus it diluted the exchange value of every dollar's worth of purchasing media in circulation. When the government receives gold coins as a payment, that transaction does not dilute the exchange value of the currency.

If a deflation of the money supply exists, the people will benefit when the government buys gold because in times of deflation the money supply should be increased. By buying gold in times of inflation of the money supply, the government increases the money supply, thus worsening the inflation unless some action is taken to offset the increase. That could be done by having the commercial banks reduce their loans of bank credit, or by having the Federal Reserve banks sell securities, or by increasing the amount of goods and services being offered for sale.

HOW DID THE GOVERNMENT PAY FOR THE GOLD IT BOUGHT?

From 1792 to 1863, the United States government "paid" for the gold it received by making the gold into gold coins and returned those coins as payment to the seller. Thus, additional coins were placed into circulation and the total money supply was increased.

From 1863 to 1933, the government paid for gold with gold coins or with gold certificates equal in face value to the exchange value of the gold. Both methods caused an increase in the amount of currency in circulation.

Between 1933 and 1968, the government paid for gold with a check issued against its account in the Federal Reserve Bank of New York. When the check was deposited in any commercial bank, the commercial bank would send it to its Federal Reserve bank and receive a bookkeeping credit for the amount. The check was then sent to the Federal Reserve Bank of New York. The Federal Reserve Bank of New York would debit the United States account and credit the account of the FederalReserve bank from which it received the check.

To make up its debit, the government would send to the Federal Reserve Bank of New York gold certificates equal in value to the check it issued as payment for the gold. The result was that the government "paid" for the gold without taxing the people for the payment. The gold was "paid" for by increasing the money supply. The demand deposits of the seller of the gold were increased. Those demand deposits are a part of the money supply. In addition to increasing the demand deposits, the Federal Reserve bank could deposit the gold certificates with Federal Reserve agent and receive four times their value in Federal Reserve notes. That would increase the money supply still more.

WHAT IS MEANT BY THE TERM "GOLD STANDARD?"

There are three types of gold standards:

1. Gold-coin standard.
2. Gold-bullion standard.
3. Gold-exchange standard.

When a nation is on a gold-coin standard it means the following:

(a) A specific number of grains of gold in the gold coins has a fixed legal tender value for the payment of each one-dollar debt.
(b) Unlimited coinage of gold coins.
(c) Unrestricted ownership and mobility of gold coins.
(d) All other currencies can be exchanged for gold coins at the fixed rate.

When a nation is on a gold-bullion standard it means that no gold coins are used as currency, but the currency in use may be exchanged for gold bullion at a set price or a set rate of exchange under certain conditions and limitations.

When a nation is on a gold-exchange standard it means that the government and the people in that country can make payments for the goods or services received from another country with currency that is equal in exchange value to a fixed exchange value of gold.

Note that the one common feature of all three types of gold standards is that the government has a set or fixed price on gold. It is for that reason that gold has not served well as a medium of exchange. It is not that gold is a poor medium of exchange. The fault lies in attempts by government officials to set a fixed price on the gold.

DO WE HAVE ENOUGH GOLD TO RETURN TO THE FULL GOLD STANDARD?

We can change all of our purchasing media into gold coins and/or certificates redeemable in gold if we do not care what price we set for the gold and at what price we are willing to exchange goods and services.

There are two ways to accomplish this. The first is to lower the price of all goods (except gold) and services to about one-fifth of present prices. (This calculation is based on the price of gold at $160 per ounce.) The second way is to raise the price of gold to about $800 an ounce.

Let us suppose that the United States possess 250 million ounces of gold and that the world price of gold is $160 per ounce. Assume, also, that we now have 200 billion dollars' worth of purchasing media in circulation in the United States. Now, if we are willing to reduce the price of all the goods and services being offered for sale to one-fifth of their present prices, the 250 million ounces of gold could be converted into coins and gold certificates and there would be enough purchasing media to exchange all the goods and services being offered for sale at the new reduced prices.

The 40 billion dollars' worth of the new all gold purchasing medium would then be equal in relation to the lower prices, as formerly the 200 billion dollars' worth of purchasing media was equal in relation to the higher prices of the goods and services. Each item would have the same exchange value in relation to every other item that it previously had. If no one had debts, people would not suffer an apparent gain or loss, except the owners of gold who would gain five times their previous buying power.

The second way to return to a full gold standard is to increase the price of gold five times the $160, i.e., to $800 per ounce, and leave all other prices as they are now. Then the 40 billion dollars' worth of gold would be worth 200 billion dollars, which is the hypothetical dollar amount of purchasing media with which we began.

This method also would not cause people to suffer an apparent gain or loss, provided no one had debts. Only the owners of gold would gain five times their previous buying power. But the non-owners of gold would suffer a serious loss of buying power (their buying power would be only one-fifth of what it was previously) when they wanted to buy gold in either of the two ways. This might explain why the owners of gold advocate that gold be used as a medium of exchange.

The point is that if we wish to have 100% of our purchasing medium in gold coins at a *fixed* price for gold, we can do it either by adjusting the price of gold or by adjusting the prices of everything else.

The above ideas have been tried many times in the past. They never worked for a long period of time without causing injustices to the non-owners of gold. Gold coins could serve as media of exchange, but when the gold standard (a fixed price) is applied to the coins, they will serve well only until the market price of gold changes.

IS IT NECESSARY THAT THE CURRENCY USED IN INTERNATIONAL TRADE BE GOLD OR SILVER?

While it may be convenient, at times, to use gold or silver as currency in international trade it is not necessary. Buying and selling is bartering. When goods or services are sold to people in another country, they can be paid for only with the goods or services of the purchasers. The only time people, other than speculators and money changers, really barter their goods or services for gold or silver is when they want gold or silver for some specific use.

If governments would stay out of all international transactions, gold and silver would be exchanged by private corporations and people in the same way other commodities are exchanged. It is the actions of governments in cooperation with international money changers that make it appear necessary to use gold or silver to carry on international trade.

DO FULL BODIED GOLD AND SILVER COINS SERVE WELL AS A MEDIUM OF EXCHANGE?

When the market value of the metal in a coin and the legal tender or the face value of the coin are equal, the coin is called a full bodied coin.

In order for any coin to serve as a medium of exchange, it must be profferable as well as acceptable. That is, the person who possesses the coin must be willing to exchange it for goods and services.

To discover how well the United States silver coins served as a medium of exchange, let us review briefly the history of their use.

The United States government first minted silver coins in 1794, declaring them to be legal tender at their face value. That was the market value of their silver content at the time they were authorized to be minted in 1792.

But after the authorization was given in 1792, the market price of silver increased about 2%. The result was that the coins then were not profferable as a medium of exchange. The people who happened to own silver coins exchanged them for their higher market value, instead of using them as a medium of exchange. Because many of the silver dollar coins were being sold for their silver content value instead of being used as media of exchange, President Jefferson in 1805 ordered the minting of the silver dollar coins stopped. No silver dollar coins were minted between 1805 and 1835.

The silver dollar coins were not really needed because bank notes were in circulation. But there was a serious shortage of fractional coins, which continued until 1853 when Congress reduced the amount of silver in the fractional silver coins by 7%.

The result of that reduction of the silver content in the

silver coins made the market value of the coins about 5% less than their legal tender or face value. Then the coins were issued in sufficient quantities and they stayed in circulation. Thus, the coins were both acceptable and profferable as media of exchange. Note, however, that they were no longer full bodied coins. The market value of their silver content was less than their legal tender value. They served as a medium of exchange at their face value because they were legal tender at their face value and were received as a payment for taxes at their face value, not because they were made of silver. The silver coins served well as a medium of exchange until the Civil War.

Shortly after the start of the Civil War the price of silver increased so that the market value of the silver in the coins was equal to and even higher than the legal tender value of the coins. Thus, the coins again became full bodied coins, and again the people refused to offer them as a medium of exchange. They were acceptable but they were not profferable. People either hoarded them or exchanged them for the higher market value of their silver content.

In place of fractional coins the people used postage stamps and fractional paper notes as media of exchange. The postage stamps and the fractional paper notes did not drive the silver coins out of circulation. The coins were acceptable but people refused to offer them as a medium of exchange.

In 1874 large deposits of silver were discovered in Nevada. The result was a drop in the price of silver so that the market price of the silver content of the coins was less than the legal tender value of the coins. Again, large quantities of silver coins were minted and circulated as a medium of exchange. People were willing to offer them and people were willing to accept them. But they were not full bodied coins.

For ninety years between 1874 and 1964, silver coins circulated as a medium of exchange in adequate amounts. During all those years, with the possible exception of very short periods, the market value of the silver content of the coins was much less than the legal tender or face value of the coins. There were times when the silver in the silver dollar coin was worth only 35 cents.

During all those years the silver coins served as a medium of exchange, they were profferable and acceptable not because they were silver coins, but because they were declared to be legal tender at a higher exchange value than the market value of their silver content.

In 1965 the market value of the silver content in the silver coins again increased so that it was above the legal tender value of the coins. The result again was the withholding of the coins as media of exchange. They were either exchanged for the higher market value of their silver content or they were kept as a store of value.

Do these experiences mean that silver coins are not desirable as a medium of exchange? No. It means that silver coins (and gold coins) are not appropriate items to serve as a medium of exchange when the government declares them to have a legal tender value which is higher or lower than the market value of their metal content.

If the government declares them to have a legal tender value that is lower than the market value of their silver content, they will not be offered as a medium of exchange. If the government declares them to have a legal tender value that is higher than the market value of their silver content, there is no need for the coins to be made of silver; they will serve as a medium of exchange just as well if they are made of nickel and/or copper, as they have since 1965.

In order to have full bodied coins serve as a medium of exchange, the government need not and should not declare them to be legal tender. But if it does, it should declare them to be legal tender at the market value of their metal content at the time the coins are used as a payment. Then the people would always be willing to offer the coins as a medium of exchange and no unjust payments would be made legal. That is what some of the states did with foreign gold and silver coins before 1853.

For the people in a country that produces gold or silver, there is a way for them to have gold or silver coins serve as a medium of exchange. But it is doubtful that a country which does not produce gold or silver can be persuaded to exchange its goods and services for gold or silver to use as a national medium of exchange when bona fide credit certificates can serve the purpose.

HOW WELL DO FULL BODIED GOLD COINS SERVE AS A MEDIUM OF EXCHANGE?

The United States government minted the first gold coins in 1795 and continued to mint them intermittently until 1933. During all those years we had unlimited coinage of gold coins. That meant that the government would buy all the gold brought to the mint and pay for it at the set legal tender value for gold coins. It meant that the government would keep the market price of gold from going lower than the set legal tender value, thus assuring that the gold coins would remain full bodied coins. These advantages, however, did not mean that the people would always use the coins as a medium of exchange.

When the market value of the gold content of the coins was higher than the legal tender value of the coins, people refused to offer them as a medium of exchange. This took place during most of the period between 1795 and 1834. During those years the government would receive the gold at the set price of $19.39 per fine ounce; but the market value varied between $19.39 and $20.60 per ounce.

In 1834, the government increased the price of gold to $20.69 per ounce. That price brought much gold to the mint because it was higher than any other market price. Then many coins were made and circulated as a medium of exchange.

In 1837, the government slightly reduced the price to

$20.67 per ounce which was still higher than the ordinary market price. So the coins circulated as a medium of exchange until the Civil War.

During the Civil War, the market price of gold went above the government-set price. The result was that gold coins were not offered as a medium of exchange, except in California where gold was being produced.

Generally speaking, after the Civil War and until the early 1930s, enough gold was produced so that the market price did not go above the $20.67 per ounce paid by the United States mint. That price paid by the mint kept the market price from going below the $20.67 per ounce. So the gold coins remained full bodied coins and stayed in circulation.

We should keep in mind, however, that if the government had not continued to buy gold for $20.67 per ounce, the market price of gold might have fallen below that price when gold was discovered in Alaska.

History shows what it is necessary to do to keep full bodied coins in circulation. Coins are not full bodied just because they are made of gold or silver. And coins do not serve as a medium of exchange just because they are full bodied or just because they are gold or silver.

About 1930 the market price of everything except gold began to fall. But the market price of gold did not decrease because the government controlled the price. The government would buy or sell gold at $20.67 per ounce. That meant that the owners of gold had a special advantage over the owners of other items. They had an asset (gold) the price of which the government would not allow to decline.

Because some people saw the advantage of owning gold and because some banks were not considered safe, some people began to redeem their gold certificates and Federal Reserve notes for gold.

Then government officials saw that they would not have enough gold with which to redeem all the currency that was redeemable for gold. So in 1933 President Roosevelt reversed the government policy pertaining to gold. That was the end of the use of gold in our domestic currency.

Let us remember that when the people tried to redeem their currency for gold coins in the early 1930s, they wanted the coins so that they could keep them as a store of value. And when coins are kept as a store of value they do not serve as a medium of exchange.

Does all this mean that full bodied gold coins would not serve well as a medium of exchange? No. It means that full bodied gold coins will not serve well as a medium of exchange if the government places a fixed value on the coins that is higher or lower than the market value of the metal content of the coins.

DO NOTES, CERTIFICATES, AND TOKEN COINS SERVE WELL AS MEDIA MEDIA OF EXCHANGE, IF THEY ARE REDEEMABLE FOR A FIXED AMOUNT OF GOLD OR SILVER AND IF THEY ARE DECLARED TO BE LEGAL TENDER AT A FIXED VALUE?

Let us review what happened when the one-dollar silver certificate was used as one of the items of our currency. The government gave a written promise on the certificate to redeem each one-dollar silver certificate for one dollar in silver, i.e., for 371.25 grains of pure silver, and also declared that each one-dollar certificate was legal tender for a one dollar payment for debts and taxes.

During the ninety years (1878 to 1968) the silver certificate served as a medium of exchange, it was not used as a medium of exchange because it was redeemable in silver. The fact that it was redeemable for 371.25 grains of silver was hardly considered because the government had also given the certificate a legal tender value of one dollar when it was used as a payment for debts and taxes. Thus, the silver certificate had two exchange values, the legal tender exchange value and the market exchange value of the 371.25 grains of silver for which it was the evidence of a claim. It was a certificate of legal tender for a one dollar payment and it was a warehouse receipt for 371.25 grains of silver.

However, by 1967 the exchange value of 371.25 grains of silver went above the one-dollar legal tender exchange value of the certificate. (Advertisements in some newspapers were offering as much as $1.60 for each one-dollar certificate.) At that time the people refused to use it as legal tender or as a medium of exchange People began to use it as the evidence of a claim for 371.25 grains of silver, and they continued such use until June 25, 1968, at which time the government stopped redeeming the certificates.

The certificates still are legal tender at their face value, but few remain in circulation because once they are redeemed, they are destroyed.

When in 1862 and 1863 United States notes were issued on which was written, "The United States of America will pay to the Bearer on Demand . . . (silver or gold) dollars," the government did not and could not make such payments because, at that time, it did not have the gold or silver dollars with which to fulfill such a demand.

If the government had been able to pay such a demand, however, people would have redeemed the notes for gold or silver and then either hoarded the metal or sold it for the market price which was then higher than the legal tender value of the coins. The notes then would have been destroyed and would no longer have served as a medium of exchange.

Token coins which are redeemable in gold or silver will be used by people just as they used silver certificates.

HOW CAN THE GOVERNMENT ISSUE NOTES, CERTIFICATES, OR WAREHOUSE RECEIPTS SO THAT THEY WILL BE REDEEMABLE IN GOLD OR SILVER AT A DECLARED LEGAL TENDER VALUE AND CONTINUE TO SERVE AS MEDIA OF EXCHANGE?

It is not necessary for government officials to declare

such items to be legal tender, but if they do, they should declare them to be legal tender for payments equal to the amount of the market value of the metal for which they are the evidence of a claim at the time they are used as payments. Then the redeemable notes, certificates, or warehouse receipts will continue to serve as media of exchange because their legal tender value and the market value of the metal for which they are the evidence of a claim will always be equal.

WHY DO WE HAVE LAWS AGAINST THE COUNTERFEITING OF COINS AND OTHER CURRENCY?

Placing counterfeit currency into circulation is an inflation of the currency in circulation. The result is an unjust increase in the price of all goods and services, and a lowering of the exchange value of every dollar's worth of currency that was earned and issued in good faith.

Or we can say that when a person buys anything with counterfeit currency, that person steals from all the owners of the bona fide currency in circulation.

DOES ARTICLE I, SECTION 10, OF THE UNITED STATES CONSTITUTION WHICH STATES, "NO STATE SHALL . . . COIN MONEY: EMIT BILLS OF CREDIT . . .," MAKE IT UNCONSTITUTIONAL FOR A STATE TO ISSUE TAX CREDIT CERTIFICATES?

At the time the Constitution was written, the people were experienced with the use of bills of credit and bills of exchange. A bill of credit was a promise to pay. It was a note. A bill of exchange was an order to pay. The United States Constitution only prevents the states from issuing bills with a promise to pay.

When a state issues a tax credit certificate, it is not coining money (making coins), nor is it issuing a bill with a promise to pay. It is issuing a document (a certificate) which it promises to receive for any payment due it. It also will redeem that certificate when it is presented as payment for the taxes levied at the time it was issued. So there is no promise to pay made by the state. We, therefore, conclude that the United States Constitution does not prevent a state from issuing tax credit certificates.

DOES ARTICLE VIII, SECTION 9, OF THE WISCONSIN CONSTITUTION WHICH STATES, "NO SCRIP, CERTIFICATE, OR OTHER EVIDENCE OF STATE DEBT, WHATSOEVER, SHALL BE ISSUED, EXCEPT FOR SUCH DEBTS AS ARE AUTHORIZED BY THE SIXTH AND SEVENTH SECTIONS OF THIS ARTICLE," PREVENT THE STATE FROM ISSUING TAX CREDIT CERTIFICATES?

A bona fide tax credit certificate is not a scrip giving evidence of a debt, it is not a certificate giving evidence of a debt, nor is it any kind of evidence of a state debt. In fact, it is issued by a state in order to make it unnecessary to issue bonds, which are evidence of debts. Thus we conclude that the Wisconsin Constitution does not prevent the legislature from authorizing the issuing of bona fide tax credit certificates.

DID ABRAHAM LINCOLN AND THE U.S. CONGRESS IN 1862 AND 1863 ISSUE THE U.S. NOTES IN ORDER TO SUPPLY THE PEOPLE WITH A MEDIUM OF EXCHANGE?

The U.S. Congress issued $450,000,000 worth of the U.S. notes to supply the government with media of exchange to avoid the taxation or the borrowing needed to pay for the war.

The government paid out these U.S. notes for its needed expenses and in turn received these notes for the payment of all obligations due it (except for interest on the federal debt and custom duties), so the people used the U.S. notes along with privately issued bank notes as their media of exchange.

However, beginning about July 1, 1863, the U.S. government began borrowing bank credit from the newly chartered private national banks and continued borrowing to pay for the balance of the cost of the war. At the end of the year 1865, the U.S. government debt was $2,678,000,000. In 1860, the year before the war began, the debt was only $65,000,000.

WHAT IS THE FEDERAL RESERVE SYSTEM?

The Federal Reserve System is not a real banking system for the American people. The Federal Reserve banks, which are a part of the Federal Reserve System, serve as banks only for their member banks and for the United States government. We must distinguish between the Federal Reserve System and the Federal Reserve banks.

We must keep in mind that the commercial banking system serving the people in the United States is called a fractional reserve banking system. It is not called the Federal Reserve Banking system, although many of the commercial banks are members of the Federal Reserve System.

The Federal Reserve System is an organizational apparatus established by Congress in 1913 to control our fractional reserve banking system. Because the commercial banks are allowed to operate on the fractional reserve banking system for demand deposits, they can cause an inflation or a deflation of bank credit. The Board of Governors, using the Federal Reserve banks and the Federal Open Market Committee as tools, are supposed to control the operations of the fractional reserve banking system for the benefit of the public. They are supposed to prevent an inflation or deflation of the money supply.

The Federal Reserve System is made up of the following:

1. The Board of Governors. (The Federal Reserve Board)

2. The Federal Open Market Committee.
3. The Federal Advisory Council.
4. The twelve Federal Reserve banks with their branches.
5. The member banks (the owners—stockholders—of the Federal Reserve banks).

The Board of Governors and the Federal Open Market Committee decide all major policies for the Federal Reserve banks.

Neither The Federal Reserve System nor its Board of Governors is a corporation. The board is a committee of men appointed by the president of the United States and approved by the United States Senate.

The Board of Governors is not the Federal Reserve banks. The Board of Governors is an independent agency of the government created by Congress.

It is the twelve Federal Reserve banks which are private corporations. All local banks with the word "national" in their title are members of the Federal Reserve System and they are the stockholders of the Federal Reserve banks. Some, but not all, state banks also are members of the Federal Reserve System.

The Federal Reserve banks serve as banks only to their member banks (the local banks) and to the United States government. Their main function is to act as instruments which the Board of Governors and the Federal Open Market Committee use to control the money supply. They also issue Federal Reserve notes in exchange for interest-bearing government bonds given to them as collateral.

The Federal Open Market Committee is made up of the Board of Governors and the presidents of the Federal Reserve banks. For details on the F.O.M.C. see chapter XII.

The Federal Advisory Council is a committee made up of one commercial banker from each of the twelve Federal Reserve districts. Its function is purely advisory.

The officials of the Board of Governors frequently

receive blame for the evils of the fractional reserve banking system for demand deposits. If blame is to go to them, it should be for not offering a plan to enable individuals and governmental bodies to obtain all the bona fide currency they need without borrowing it. Then they would really be serving the public interest because then the commercial banks could operate their demand deposit accounts on a 100% reserve banking system.

CAN THE PEOPLE THEMSELVES, WITHOUT ANY ACTION BY GOVERNMENT OFFICIALS, AVOID THE USE OF FEDERAL RESERVE NOTES?

If the people will accept only coins or checks, instead of Federal Reserve notes when receiving a payment or when receiving change, Federal Reserve notes will have no takers. Therefore, they will not circulate as currency.

It is not necessary for the people to use Federal Reserve notes, because Congress has authorized the Treasury Department to mint as many coins as are needed. All the people have to do is ask for the coins at their bank.

It is only a slight inconvenience to carry up to $50 in coins. Larger payments can be made with checks, including American Express Travelers Cheques.

CAN THE PEOPLE THEMSELVES, WITHOUT ANY ACTION BY GOVERNMENT OFFICIALS, STOP THE OPERATIONS OF THE FEDERAL RESERVE BANKS?

The people can give all their banking business to banks that are not members of the Federal Reserve System and use coins instead of Federal Reserve notes. Then the Federal Reserve banks will have only a limited demand for their services. That limited service can be provided by some of the regular banks and the United States Treasury Department in the same manner as was done before the Federal Reserve banks existed. This action will not mean that the local member banks will be put out of business. It will be a strong encouragement for them to become state non-member banks.

The Federal Reserve banks are owned by the member banks. When all the member banks withdraw from the Federal Reserve System, the Federal Reserve banks will have no owners and their surplus funds will be given to the United States Treasury.

At the present time more non-member banks are doing business in the United States than member banks, although the member banks have more assets and liabilities than the non-member banks.

WOULD WE HAVE A TRUSTWORTHY "MONEY SYSTEM" IF WE NO LONGER USED THE FEDERAL RESERVE BANKS AND THE FEDERAL RESERVE NOTES?

Assuming that we did nothing else, we would have the same "money problems" (bank failures, inflations, deflations, booms and busts, unemployment, and ever increasing interest-bearing debts) that existed before the Federal Reserve System was established and that still exist. These are the problems the Federal Reserve System was supposed to prevent. We know that it did not. We also know that interest-bearing debts increased almost beyond comprehension.

To have a trustworthy "money system" we must gradually replace the fractional reserve banking system with a 100% reserve banking system for demand deposits in commercial banks. (See chapter XI for details.)

HOW CAN A BANK MAKE ANY LOANS IF IT IS REQUIRED TO OPERATE ON A 100% RESERVE REQUIREMENT SYSTEM?

Commercial banks have two departments that serve its depositors:

1. The department for demand deposit accounts.
2. The department for time and savings accounts.

When a depositor places his funds in a time or savings account, he expects the bank to loan out those funds. He should not expect the bank to return his funds on demand.

The bank has rules and regulations to which the depositor agrees when he makes a deposit in a savings account. The following are the rules and regulations regarding withdrawals in a pass-book issued by the savings department of a large bank in Milwaukee, Wisconsin.

> NOTICE OF WITHDRAWAL. The bank reserves the right to require a thirty-day prior notice in writing of depositor's intention to withdraw any sum not exceeding One Hundred Dollars, a sixty day prior notice in writing of the depositor's intention to withdraw any sum in excess of One Hundred Dollars up to Five Hundred Dollars, and a ninety day prior notice in writing of depositors intention to withdraw any sum in excess of Five Hundred Dollars.

The banks pay interest on time and savings deposits, so they in turn have a right to loan out those funds in order to earn the interest and make a profit. So it should not be expected and it is not necessary for the bank to have any reserves for time and savings accounts, especially when a bank has rules such as those above for withdrawals. Mutual savings banks are not required to keep any reserves for depositors' savings accounts.

Therefore, when we speak of a 100% reserve system, we are not referring to the time and savings deposit accounts, we are only referring to the demand deposit accounts. The depositor of demand deposits does not loan his funds to the bank. In many cases those are the funds the bank loaned to the depositor. In those cases the depositor is paying interest on those funds. He has a right to expect the bank to keep those funds on hand until he demands them by his check. He does not expect the bank to loan those same funds to someone else.

We should consider it normal for the banks to be able to pay out their demand deposits in full, on demand. But they will be able to do that only when they operate on a 100% reserve system.

WHY SHOULD CERTIFICATES IN LIEU OF COINS BE ISSUED, INSTEAD OF UNITED STATES NOTES, TO REPLACE FEDERAL RESERVE NOTES AND DEMAND DEPOSITS OF BANK CREDIT?

A note is the written evidence of a promise to pay with something of value. A bona fide note will specify the item to be paid. Honesty requires that we state the item to be paid and the intention to keep that promise. If the government issues a note without a promise to pay or with a promise to pay without stating the item to be paid, such a promise is meaningless and should not be issued by government officials.

The coins we are now using are not the evidence of promises to pay. They are the evidence of the law passed by Congress which states "All coins and currencies . . . shall be legal tender . . ." Therefore, certificates in lieu of coins would serve as coins do in giving the evidence of that law.

It would be more appropriate to use such certificates to replace Federal Reserve notes and demand deposits of bank credit, than it would be to use United States notes which are supposed to be the evidence of promises to pay, but which are not.

An important lesson can be learned from our experience with silver certificates. From 1886 to 1967, most of our one-dollar bills were silver certificates. They had their exchange value and were used as currency because they were declared to be legal tender at their face value, not because they were redeemable for 371.25 grains of silver.

For nearly all those years, the 371.25 grains of silver was worth between 35 cents and 90 cents and the legal tender value was worth $1. Those silver certificates, like the coins were evidence of legal tender.

It was only when the price of the 371.25 grains of silver went above one dollar that the people did not use the certificate as the evidence of legal tender. They redeemed it for the silver.

The president, the members of Congress, and the Board of Governors of the Federal Reserve System, all of whom are responsible for our money system, would have served the public interest if, at the time the 371.25 grains of silver became worth one dollar, they replaced the silver certificates with certificates in lieu of coins. Instead, they allowed the Federal Reserve banks to replace them with Federal Reserve notes which are based on government debts.

WHAT ITEMS WOULD SERVE AS INTERNATIONAL CURRENCY?

There are two types of items which will serve internationally as media of exchange:

1. Items with exchange value in themselves, commodites.
2. Certificates or other documents giving evidence that the bearer has a just claim for items with exchange value, bills of exchange, certificates of credit, and warehouse receipts.

To make the above items more acceptable internationally, they may be warranted by internationally recognized organizations or corporations.

The items that will serve internationally as media of exchange are the same items that will serve nationally as media of exchange. If the above items were used internationally as media of exchange and if government officials in all countries did not interfere with the free exchanging of goods and currencies, balance of payments deficits or surpluses would never occur. The buying and selling would be like bartering and in bartering, no one can sell any more or any less than he can buy.

WHAT TYPE OF UNEMPLOYMENT IS CAUSED BY A SHORTAGE OF THE MEDIA OF EXCHANGE IN CIRCULATION?

Every productively employed person is producing a product or performing a service for a customer. If the quality and price of the product or service are satisfactory to enough customers and if those customers have sufficient media of exchange, the product or service will be sold and the person will continue to be employed.

Some years ago, when testifying before a Congressional committee which was inquiring about the methods to be used to create jobs, a businessman told the committee,

> In a private enterprise economy, it is business activity (the production and distribution of wanted goods and services) undertaken in the expectation of profits which creates jobs. If the profits are realized, the jobs continue and perhaps grow in number. If the profits are not realized, the jobs and the companies which offer them eventually disappear. There will be virtually no unused capacity in either manpower or material resources when the possibility can be seen for employing them at a profit.

Employers do not manufacture jobs. They, together with their employees, manufacture products and perform services. The employer and the employee are both working for the customer. The customers, in the end, pay the wages of the employees and the profits of the employer.

To enable the customers to buy the goods and services produced, the amount of media of exchange in circulation must be no less than the amount needed to maintain a stable general price level.

A stable general price level would be maintained if bona fide certificates of credit issued by the possessors of the goods or services being offered for sale, and/or bona fide tax credit or tax payment certificates issued by governmental bodies, were used as media of exchange. Coins can be issued by governmental bodies as tax credit certificates.

Because those items can be issued without incurring any interest-bearing debts, they can be issued in the quantity needed. Because they are redeemable in goods or services or as payments for taxes, no one can honestly issue them in too great a quantity. So no deflation or inflation of the media of exchange need occur. Thus, the right amount of the media of exchange can be placed in circulation and a stable general price level will be achieved.

In the past as well as at the present time the single most unstabilizing factor of the general price level was and is the fact that all of the items (except our coins) that we use as media of exchange come into circulation only as a result of a governmental body, a private corporation, or an individual incurring interest-bearing debts. The items which serve as media of exchange should be brought into circulation, not in relation to the amount of interest-bearing debts incurred, but in relation to the amount of goods and services being offered for sale.

When people, including government officials, speak of creating more jobs, they should identify the products to be made, the services to be rendered, the debts to be incurred, the wages to be paid, and the profits for the employers. If the wage rates, the interest rates, and the profits are higher than the customers are willing and able to pay, the products and the services will not be bought and no employment will be available.

We must keep in mind that there is more than one reason for people to be unemployed. The reason for one person's unemployment may be different from another's.

When there is general unemployment, i.e., unemployment not limited to specific groups, and the general price level for all goods and services is low or declining, we can conclude that the cause of that general unemployment is due to a shortage of the items that serve as media of exchange. This was the condition that existed in the United States in the 1930's. All our natural resources, tools, energy, knowledge, and willingness to work were to no avail.

When there is limited unemployment, i.e., certain specific groups of people are unemployed, and the general price level of all goods and services is stable or increasing, we can conclude that this type of unemployment is not due to a shortage of the media of exchange in circulation. This is the condition we had in 1976. So what is the reason for this type of unemployment?

To determine the reason, we must learn why certain groups of people are unemployed. Who are the individuals or groups of individuals that are unemployed? If we do a little studying, I think we shall find that the unemployed are:

1. Those who build houses.
2. Those who build automobiles.
3. Those who make any product or render any service at a price that is higher than many people are willing or able to pay.
4. Those who have not yet acquired the knowledge, the skill, or the willingness to earn the government set legal minimum wage.
5. Those who are prevented from working by government laws, such as those declaring that a person is too old or too young to be employed.
6. Those who are being paid enough when they do not work so that they do not have a desire to work.
7. Those who are for various reasons temporarily unemployed, about 3% or 4%.

These, perhaps are the main classifactions of those who are unemployed in the United States at the present time. To put these people to work requires a different solution for each group.

Because we know that the general price level of all goods and services is increasing at the present time, we know that the people in these seven groups are not unemployed because of a shortage of media of exchange in circulation. So if the amount of the media of exchange in circulation were abnormally increased, an abnormal increase of the general price level of all the goods and services being offered for sale would occur. That is not the solution.

In order that the people in these seven categories have productive employment, it is necessary that those in groups 1, 2, and 3 reduce the price of the product or service they are selling to a price which more customers are willing and able to pay.

To give employment to the people in groups 4 and 5, government officials should repeal those state and federal laws which prevent an employer from hiring workers on terms that are mutually agreeable to the employer and the employee.

At the present time it is illegal for an employer to give employment to people in groups 4 and 5 on terms which will permit the employer to stay in business.

People are human beings. They are free agents. They are responsible for their own acts. They are neither wards nor servants of government officials. They are not commodities to be bought or sold. But the goods produced and the services rendered by people are items of commerce. They are items with an exchange value. And in the free enterprise economic system the price or exchange value of goods and services and the conditions under which the goods and services are to be exchanged should be determined by mutual agreement between the buyer and seller and not by government officials.

To give employment to the people in group 6, government officials should repeal state and federal laws that require people to be paid about as much to do nothing as they might earn if they worked.

Those in group 7 are making adjustments in their employment and will in time take care of themselves. Many of them are just changing jobs.

If we should ever have general unemployment with a drop in the general price level of all goods and services, we can conclude that unemployment of such magnitude is probably due to a shortage of the media of exchange in circulation.

One solution for that kind of unemployment is to increase the amount of media of exchange in circulation to an amount that will bring the general price level up to what it was before the unemployment began. The other solution is to reduce all prices and wages to conform to the decreased amount of media of exchange in circulation.

CAN OUR MONEY SYSTEM BE USED TO CAUSE GENERAL UNEMPLOYMENT?

When a person obtains employment, he is selling or exchanging his services for a certain number of dollars' worth of the money supply for each unit of time he works or for each unit of the product he makes. The price of each unit of his time or each unit of his product is, to a great extent, determined by the total money supply in circulation.

If the money supply is increased, there will be a greater effective demand for his time or his product. He may be able to obtain more dollars' worth of the money supply for each unit of his time or product.

On the other hand, if the money supply in circulation is decreased, his share of it will be decreased. To be fully employed, he must work the same number of hours or produce the same number of units of his product for his reduced share of the money supply. There is not enough dollars' worth of the money supply available for him to sell the same number of units of his time or his products at the previous price.

If he does not reduce the price of his product or his services to adapt to the reduced money supply in circulation, he will be unemployed or only partly employed. In order to sell his goods or services, the price must be adjusted to match the increase and the decrease of the money supply. If he does not increase the price of his goods or services when the money supply is increased, he will not have enough goods or services to meet the demand. If he does not decrease the price of his goods or services when the money supply is decreased, he will not be able to sell the same amount of goods or services he formerly sold.

These are the basic principles underlying the causes of general employment or general unemployment. There would be no general unemployment if the prices of goods and services were reduced at the same time and at the same rate that the money supply was reduced.

Prices for goods and services can usually be increased when the money supply is increased, but because of long term contracts it is difficult to lower the prices for goods and services when the money supply is decreased.

Once we are aware of the fact that the real cause of general unemployment is due to an imbalance between the money supply and the general price level of goods and services, we will know how to correct it: We must either increase the money supply or decrease the prices of the goods and services being offered for sale. At the present time, the people who produce our goods and services do not control the money supply, so they cannot increase it without incurring interest-bearing debts. They can only reduce their prices and wages.

If they decrease their prices and wages to match the decreased money supply, and the money supply is again decreased, they will again have to decrease their prices and wages or be unemployed. This reveals that when the producers and distributors of goods and services do not control the money supply, they do not fully control their own prices, wages, and employment. Their prices, wages and employment are dictated by those who control the money supply.

One congressman on a television program in March

reported that the actions taken by the Federal serve Board during the months of January and February 1975, caused a 24 billion dollar reduction in the money supply. That caused a reduction in the demand for goods and services, which in turn caused a reduction of employment.

Such occurrences would not take place if the people who produce and exchange goods and services had full control of the items they use as media of exchange. They could issue and use certificates of credit as their media of exchange and thus be free from the control of a governmentally appointed board with power over their prices, wages, and employment.

INDEX

THE GREAT COOKIE JAR
By
Edward E. Popp

QUANTITY PRICE LIST

1 copy:	$1.95 each	25–49 copies:	$ .90 each
2–4 copies:	1.50 each	50–99 copies:	.80 each
5–9 copies:	1.25 each	100 copies:	.70 each
10–24 copies:	1.00 each		

Wisconsin residents add 4% sales tax.

Use the following order form.

Wisconsin Education Fund Date________
P. O. Box 321
Port Washington, Wisconsin 53074
Please send me ____ copies of **THE GREAT COOKIE JAR.**

Payment of $ ____ is enclosed (send check or money order).

(Please print name and address.)

Name ________________________________

Address ______________________________

City or P.O. ___________________________

State ______________________ Zip __________

Make checks payable to Wisconsin Education Fund.